Learning through art

and artefacts

KATE STEPHENS

Series Editor Margaret Morgan

Hodder & Stoughton

A MEMBER OF THE HODDER HEADLINE

British Library Cataloguing in Publication Data

A catalogue for this title is available from the British Library

ISBN 0 340

First published 1994
Impression number   10 9 8 7 6 5 4 3 2 1
Year   1999   1998   1997   1996   1995   1994

Typeset by Wearset, Boldon, Tyne and Wear.
Printed in Great Britain for Hodder & Stoughton Educational, a division of
Hodder Headline Plc, 338 Euston Road, London NW1 3BH by
Scotprint Ltd, Musselburgh

Contents

Series preface: *Art and design for learning*   5

Preface   9

Acknowledgements   13

1   Learning through art and artefacts   15

    Introduction   15
    The role of the teacher   16
    What can be gained through learning about art?   21
    Using the works of others   25

2   The value of original works of art   30

    Sources of art and artefacts   30
    Museums and galleries   31
    Artists in residence and school-based workshops   36
    Local education authority and/or museum loan schemes   43
    The use of secondary source material   45
    Advantages of resource material   46

3   Ideas in action   50

    A Diwali ceremonial project   50
    An artists' and craftworkers' day   53
    A museum visit within an integrated project   55
    Using the environment   58

4   Timing the introduction of artefacts   63

    Using artefacts at the beginning of a project   63
    Using artefacts in the middle of a project   64
    An end in itself   66
    Activities from the classroom   69
    A case study   74

5   Art into language – language into art   80

   Using the spoken word   82
   Stories within pictures and other artefacts   83

6   Implementation and development   88

   Reviewing the place of artefacts in our curriculum   88
   Who, where, what?   91

Bibliography   95

Colour section – children's art from four to eleven   97

Series preface: Art and design for learning

Art and design for learning is a series of books which aims to provide a number of individuals involved in teaching with a platform for which to write about working with children and the thinking which lies behind their work.

The series authors are all experienced teachers and educationalists. They have had the privilege of visiting and working in schools, or of working with groups of teachers who have generously given permission for their children's work, and some of their own thoughts, to be included.

In the present climate of intense curriculum development created by the introduction of the National Curriculum for England and Wales, there is a great fear amongst some teachers that room for individuality and inventiveness is in danger of being lost. If this were to be the case, it would of course be disastrous, but it need not happen.

Research historians and cooks experimenting with fifteenth- and seventeenth-century bread and cake recipes encountered failure until they realised that the key ingredient was never listed. This was because all the practitioners knew it to be such a basic necessity that everyone concerned would already know about it. The unlisted ingredient was yeast.

The same principle could be applied to many of our curriculum documents. The yeast in art and design education must surely be the life, energy and individuality of the child and the teacher, working creatively with the ingredient of experience and the means. Any defined curriculum agreed upon by others and presented to an establishment, an authority, county or state is inclined to appear restrictive at first glance, especially if we personally have not been responsible for drafting it. What we are able to do with it will depend on whether we see it as a platform to work from, or a cage to be imprisoned in.

It is therefore very important to coolly appraise the nature and content of the work we are undertaking with the children in our schools and to think carefully about our personal philosophy and values. We need to identify areas of any imposed curriculum that we are in fact already covering and then consider those which call for development or may need to be introduced. It is only when we really understand the common denominator which lies behind these areas of experience that we can assimilate them into a holistic and coherent developmental pattern on which to base our strategies for practice.

In simple terms, any sound curriculum pertaining to art, craft and design must surely require a broad, balanced, developmental programme which has coherence and respects the experience, strengths and weaknesses of individual children, thereby enabling them to think, respond and act for themselves. Perhaps the real evaluation of a good teacher is to see whether children can proceed with their learning independently when he/she is no longer responsible for them.

The curriculum should make it possible to introduce children to the wonders and realities of the world in which we all live and should include art, craft and design forms from our own and other cultures and times. These can prove to be an enriching experience and can broaden the children's expectation of the nature of human response together with some experience of different ways of making art and design forms.

The curriculum should enable children to see the potential, and master the practice, of any relevant technologies, from the handling of simple hand tools to the world of information technology. It should enable them to work confidently in group and class situations as well as individually: thinking, making, appraising and modifying the work they are undertaking, negotiating skilfully with one another and discussing or talking about what they are doing, or have done. All of these aspects of education can be seen in the context of the National Curriculum which has, in the main, been based on some of the best practices and experience of work in recent years.

Intimations of the yeast component are clearly apparent in these selected extracts from *Attainment Targets and Programmes of Study for Key Stages 1 and 2*. (It is also very interesting to note the clear differences in requirements between the two stages; at seven and at eleven years of age. Stage 2 assimilates and develops Stage 1 requirements, building on them developmentally with specific additions.) At Key Stage 1 (seven years) the operative words are:

> investigating, making, observing, remembering, imagining, recording, exploring, responding, collecting, selecting, sorting, recreating, recognising, identifying, *beginning* to make connections . . . [my italics].

There is a very strong emphasis throughout on *direct experience, looking at* and *talking about.* At Key Stage 2 (eleven years) the following expectations are added:

> communicating ideas and feelings, developing ideas, experimenting [there is a subtle difference between exploration and conscious experimentation], applying knowledge, planning and making, choosing appropriate materials, adapting and modifying, comparing, looking for purposes, discussing . . .

What could be clearer in suggesting a lively educational experience? I believe that individuality and inventiveness are firmly based on having the right attitudes and they usually thrive best in the context of vehicles such as interest, happenings and the building up of enthusiasm and powerful motivation. The overall structure, balance and developmental nature of any sound curriculum model can allow content to flourish in lively interaction between children, teachers and the world of learning experiences.

If we persist in hardening the content of the National Curriculum in such a way that we are not able to manoeuvre or respond to the living moment, then we have ourselves forged the links of the chain which binds us.

The books in this series do not aim to be comprehensive statements about particular areas of art, craft and design experience, but they are vigorous attempts to communicate something of the personal, convinced practice of a number of enthusiastic professionals. We hope that they will also offer enough information and guidance for others to use some of the approaches as springboards for their own exploration and experience in the classroom.

Preface

Learning through art and artefacts is about the educational potential and practice of introducing and working from art, craft and design forms with young children. This is not a new concept, indeed much valuable developmental work has been going on in schools, art centres, galleries and museums for a number of years, well before the National Curriculum was conceived. There is no doubt that the National Curriculum requirements in the context of 'Knowledge and Understanding' has sharpened our thinking about this area of experience, and I know that there are many teachers who find the 'End of Key Stage Statements' very daunting.

The development of visual literacy and knowledge and understanding of art, craft and design including the history of art, our diverse artistic heritage and a variety of other artistic traditions, together with the ability to make practical connections between this and the pupil's own work.

Hopefully this book will play its part in showing that, in reality, this experience can be vibrant and exciting and has potential in its own right, interacting with 'Investigating and Making', and carrying many cross-curricular possibilities. It is also a splendid vehicle for pupils and teachers to learn together, being unafraid to cover new ground. What better way to begin than to foster confidence in looking and responding in a personal way. The questions and practical experience can be built up from that point.

When considered coolly, it really is very surprising that in the past we did not see the potential of the experiences which could be gained by introducing even our youngest children to art and design forms. If, as teachers, we look at our own childhood learning in the primary years, we had little if any experience of this nature at all, and even at secondary level there may well be a large proportion who had sparse curriculum involvement.

With regard to the primary school, it is quite possible that one, if not the major, reason for us not having used artefacts was that some of the most prestigious art educators believed that it was inappropriate to show children pictures in the context of art, other than of their own making. The belief in the validity of the child's personal imagery was, and hopefully still is, very strong, but whereas Franz Cizek, for example, working at the turn of the century could guard his pupils' visual intake, we are in a very different position today. Our children are bombarded from the moment of birth by a host of images, and continue to be swamped throughout their lives. Television, film, video, photography, illustrated books and magazines, advertising of every scale and kind, cartoons and packaging, all build up to a huge conglomerate. We are not dealing any more with 'pure and unsullied vision', but a range of good, bad and indifferent visual experiences which I believe undoubtedly affect the child's expectation and imagery. How much more important for us to extend the range, and to introduce children to the finest 'documents' of the past and present available, in the form of two- and three-dimensional fine art, decorative and functional designed forms, buildings, environmental projects and the like, together with opportunities to meet artists, craftworkers and designers, and to begin to understand their ways of thinking and working. The proof of the pudding is in the eating, as the old addage goes, and it is very interesting to note that the teachers who have worked in this way, and have understood the real potential and developmental value of this approach are only too eager to take it further. In this book, by looking at the work and listening to what children have to say, we can see evidence of involvement as well as qualitative developmental practice.

Kate Stephens is an art and design advisory teacher working in Suffolk. Her role gives her the privilege of working with children and teachers, and covers the complete school age and ability range, including nursery. She is a strong believer in the importance of integrity in the teaching and learning experience, and spends much of her time supporting teachers as they build up curricula structured on children's understanding and imagery, and the nature and processes of art and design. Her enthusiasm is infectious, and she has a very clear understanding of the qualities which can be engendered when children are offered stimuli and resources for realistic challenge.

Both Kate and the teachers whose work is included in this book have obviously enjoyed being able to celebrate the examples of interesting practice presented here. The really telling outcomes are seen by the fact that the projects shown are only steps along the road to discovery. I sincerely hope that this book will prove to be of interest to those who are already working in this way, and to teachers who are less sure of their own practice and where the initial steps might lead. The approach is based on the skills many teachers already possess and calls for resourceful introduction of works of art and design, stimulation by means of enabling children to look and experience, and building up dialogue by means of open-ended questioning and listening. It is quite difficult to find a teacher who has not been profoundly surprised by what children have had to say about what they think or feel, and this can apply to all ages and abilities. Happily, the kind of interaction engendered in this kind of learning can be self-rewarding, and it is likely that we have not only enabled children to understand and make use of further dimensions in their own practice, but that we may well have opened up a realm of enquiry and enjoyment which could last a lifetime.

Margaret Morgan, Art Education Consultant

Acknowledgements

I would like to thank the teachers and pupils from the following Suffolk schools who have kindly allowed me to use their work in this book:

Tollgate CP; Westgate CP; Cockfield CEVP; Whitton CP; Glemsford CP; Pot Kiln CP; Great Whelnetham CEVP; Laureate CP; The Freeman CP; St Gregory and St Peter CEVP; Beyton Middle School; Chantry CJ; Laxfield CP; Stratford St Mary CP; Beacon Hill Special School; Chantry HS and Farlingaye HS; Guildhall Feoffment CP and Barrow CEVP.

My thanks also to Val Burnett of All Saints Middle School for permission to show her work; to 'Sharing in Art' for allowing me to photograph them during a workshop; to Benedict and Hannah Stephens for the use of their images; and to Vernon Place for his photograph of children at Laureate School.

Particular gratitude is due to Christine Furness of Pot Kiln School for extensive use of her work; and to Silke Miles of Chantry CJ School for her diary of events recording the use of the 'Birthday Party' by Chagall; also to Anna Wyatt and Jo Cross.

I am indebted to Ray Petty and Tim Wilson for having been kind and generous mentors whilst I have learned and gained experience in the primary classroom during the last five years; and to Margaret Morgan for her wise questions and thoughtful comments made during the writing of this book.

Finally, my special thanks to Gordon Stephens for the many hours spent on my behalf at the computer keyboard and for his help in the control of my frequent lapses into unrestrained verbosity.

This book is dedicated to Benedict and Hannah with my love.

1 Learning through art and artefacts

INTRODUCTION

I am absolutely convinced of the value of working with art and artefacts with young children. If I have a personal regret, it is that my own primary schooling failed to embrace such experiences, for I now know just how much even the very youngest pupils can gain from working in this context. Happily, ideas have changed and are changing further; children no longer have to wait until the secondary phase of their education to encounter original works of art and designed forms. This book seeks to define some aspects of the developments occurring and to suggest how we, as teachers, might extend our use of images and objects in the primary classroom.

As a child I loved looking at pictures, but it was not until my teenage years that I was enabled to become excited and informed by the visual world. If asked, I would find it easy to write an article on 'My Best Teacher', for it was identifiably 'Tommy' Tomlinson who shaped my future. She unlocked many doors for us pupils and yet had the wisdom to stand back, leaving us to decide whether or not we wished to pass through them. She was passionate about the fine arts in particular and gave us the confidence to say 'I like this' and 'I don't like that', together with the knowledge and understanding to say why in each instance.

> 'Choose, make decisions,' she would say, 'It doesn't matter if you hate something, but at least have the intelligence to ask yourself why you have that response. Only by recognising what you dislike can you truly appreciate that which has meaning for you.'
> (Anne Tomlinson)

As adults, we can enjoy the experience of looking at works of art and design in the certain knowledge that our individual and personal responses are not subject to censorship or questioning. Our feelings may be elusive and difficult to define, fleeting or profound, but they are our own, and we do not have to justify ourselves. As with music, dance, poetry and drama, art can speak directly to the heart, and if our education has helped us to look and really see, then our responses will be greatly enriched.

THE ROLE OF THE TEACHER

Children encountering a work of art or design have equal rights with adults; their responses are as real, as varied and as valid. They do not have inferior versions of mature, adult reflections, just different ones. Their reactions are often direct and immediate and should always be valued.

With this in mind, teachers have an important part to play in encouraging children to look and respond with confidence, thereby enabling deeper understanding. By encouraging questioning, suggesting possible explanations and developing sensitivities, teachers will help pupils to develop their personal responses through knowledge and insight.

Some time ago, when working with a group of teachers, a primary school colleague wrote a delightful essay on 'Real Art in the Primary School'. In her writing she offered the following definition of the teacher's task when sharing a painting with the class.

> ... the teacher must play a vital role as mediator, as discussion partner, as provider of information and explanations. Content of the picture, colour, composition, its context in historic events, techniques, the painter's sources of inspiration can all be valuable starting points for a teaching programme. But so are the children's reactions to the picture, their own experiences and ideas ...

This balance between teacher and pupil viewpoints is the key. Opinions and feelings become an interchange, and provide a wonderful forum for debate, It may be useful to view the content of such debate in terms of the following points, as together they can provide a very powerful and valid reason for teaching, using works of art, craft and design. Even more importantly, they allow children to make sense of their learning experiences.

Reasons for using art and artefacts

By using works of art pupils can:

- gain confidence when making their own personal responses;
- learn to look for reasons to think critically;
- become sensitised to the world around them;
- discover their own way of seeing through encountering artists' and designers' work;
- discover that their own work can be a safe place to express emotion and feeling;
- assimilate ideas, approaches and techniques and use them in their own work;
- gain a positive attitude towards being adventurous and experimental in their own making and doing;
- verify that ideas don't always succeed or satisfy at the first attempt;
- understand that human beings have always made art and that it is a basic human urge and not the idiosyncratic whim of the class teacher;
- encounter excellence and understand quality through seeing a wide variety of art and design forms;
- become aware of the qualities in works of art and design leading them towards becoming discerning consumers;
- talk, discuss and develop a critical vocabulary and sense of judgement;
- learn to read content and look for the story of an image or artefact;
- experience enjoyment and pleasure.

Teachers will need to decide which of these points they accept or reject and evolve a rationale tailored to match the needs of their individual school, classroom and pupils and the current ethos of the school. Further points could be added to this list by those who have discovered other valuable aspects of working through art and artefacts.

Feelings, opinions and knowledge

Many primary teachers are nervous about teaching art and feel insecure because of their lack of knowledge about the subject. My own personal experience has proved that this is a groundless fear, providing that we are willing to question our own responses and learn with the children.

It would be difficult to find any teacher who feels incapable of undertaking language development work with their class because they are unable to give a lecture on Beowolf or write a dissertation on the metaphysical poets, although they can enjoy reading them. Equally, we do not deem ourselves to be inept teachers of mathematics because we cannot expound on Pythagoras' belief that numbers are the key to the understanding of the universe. So if we can feel secure in our teaching of English, maths and science, we should feel just as confident with regard to our teaching of art, even when we wish to make references to the works of others. In the introduction to Professor E.H. Gombrich's book *The Story of Art,* he wisely points out the dangers of possessing knowledge to the exclusion of personal response, which can be debilitating rather than helpful. He says:

> ... knowing something of this history [of art, architecture, painting and sculpture] helps us to understand why artists worked in a particular way, or why they aimed at certain effects. Most of all it is a good way of sharpening our eyes for the particular characteristics of works of art, and of thereby increasing our sensitivity to the finer shades of difference ...

Yet he very straightforwardly points out that it is better to really look at something than to be able to accurately label it:

> ... but to look at a picture with fresh eyes and to venture on a voyage of discovery into it is a far more difficult but also a much more rewarding task. There is no telling what one might bring home from such a journey.

In a recent interview with Sue Lawley on Desert Island Discs, Professor Gombrich sounded surprised when she asked him if he was pleased that young children should see important works of art and know something of the history of art. He said it was far more important that children should be able to see many different kinds of pictures and be allowed to respond to them in a personal and feeling way rather than to know 'facts' and be told what they should think.

If such an eminent art historian can feel this to be the case, then we should all gain reassurance about the validity of our own responses to imagery and about our right to offer these to children. It also reaffirms the importance of exploring children's own responses with them, and the value of nurturing their reactions to the visual world.

Follow your instincts

Primary teachers are usually adept at knowing which stories will appeal to the children in their care. Prose and poetry are selected because they exemplify particular qualities that the teacher considers pertinent to planned work and which link to current projects. A range of sources is automatically reviewed for possible usage – books, magazines, ancient journals, diaries, local archives and newspapers. It becomes second nature to sort and sift until suitable pieces are found for specific purposes or characteristics: an amusing use of alliteration, a stunning example of evocative vocabulary, a compelling storyline, or sensitive descriptions of mood, atmosphere or feelings.

At best, choices are made that match the pupils' age and level of maturity and enable the intended teaching to take place. Occasionally something surprises us by failing to generate much response; conversely a chosen piece sometimes enthralls beyond all expectation. This is a healthy situation, for we should not be arbiters of children's taste and should take care not to restrict their diet through our own preferences or prejudices.

Confidence can be developed by approaching art works in a similarly open-minded manner. It is important to trust one's own instincts and to remember to offer as broad a range of art and artefacts as possible, whilst always being open to the fact that children can learn as much from looking at works which they dislike as those to which they respond favourably, providing they are given opportunities to think through these responses. Our job, as teachers, is to ask what a particular art session is going to be about, what the teaching is aiming to reveal to pupils, and will the images or objects support, extend and challenge the children's understanding?

See, for example, Figures 1(a)–(c) which show some of the work accomplished by ten- and eleven-year-old pupils involved in making studies of sleeping or resting figures. The purpose was to use line in an expressive and descriptive manner whilst drawing the human form. After the drawings were made, the teacher showed them Henry Moore's wartime shelter drawings and underground sleeper studies (see, for example, Figure 1(d) on page 21) and the children then re-worked some of their own drawings with wax crayons and drawing inks just as Moore himself might have done.

Figures 1(a)–(c) Sleeping figures related to the work on Henry Moore

Figure 1(a)

Simple starting points are sufficient, such as the ones given below, but there are, of course, many other stimuli:

- We are currently working on colour and thinking particularly about greens; can I find a landscape which records this aspect of the countryside for use in class discussion?
- We have been doing some work on mark-making; can I now locate a range of drawings that show lively and varied uses of media to share with the class when we reflect back on what has been achieved?
- Can I select appropriate lengths of fabric to discover where and how repeat patterns occur to help us in our pattern-making work?

Figure 1(h)

Figure 1(c)

Pink and Green Sleepers 1941 Tate Gallery

Figure 1(d)

WHAT CAN BE GAINED THROUGH LEARNING ABOUT ART?

Perhaps the most basic but valuable question to ask your pupils is what they think art is. This will inevitably lead on to discussion about: Who makes art? Why do they make it? When did they make it? From what do they make it? Where do we find it?

21

If these questions are handled sensitively, we can show children how learning about art can make a difference to them. In practical sessions, children are constantly exploring different ways of using colour, line, texture, form and pattern (the elements of art) within their own work. The understanding they gain through this can in turn lead them to see how the work of other people can help to further develop and extend their own making and doing. They also see many different ways of communicating and expressing a wider variety of subject matter, which in turn will help them to see their own world with new expectations and new vision.

Pupils can readily learn that art has many different facets, and even the youngest can begin to group types of work. Teachers may wish to involve pupils in categorising imagery, structures and objects as a way of understanding this fact. This could include looking at:

- paintings which tell a story or record an event;
- pictures which express an idea, mood or feeling;
- sculpture which describes character or movement;
- forms designed to hold something;
- design forms which fulfil a need;
- fabrics made to have different properties or purposes;
- buildings designed for a purpose;
- details which make a building interesting;
- items used to decorate ourselves;
- posters, prints and drawings that please or make us think.

From these kinds of collections it becomes possible to introduce the idea that different work is produced for different reasons and that artists' and designers' intentions vary according to context and circumstances.

Learning about other people's art is not meant to be a passive activity for pupils. It should involve them actively looking, feeling, finding out and making responses. It is about gathering ideas and inspiration, finding connections between themselves and others, and discovering how they can find ways forward in their own thinking and making. It is certainly not to do with pupils acquiring a body of academic knowledge on which to be tested later! It is experience

Figure 2 A nine-year-old girl designs her own Christmas wrapping paper after looking at many Christmas cards and seasonal ephemera. It seems as though she has absorbed many familiar images and kaleidoscoped them together into a wonderful piece of obsessive pattern making

which can be turned to good use, and if handled skillfully, may well promote a positive change in the children's own way of thinking.

A reception teacher sat on the carpet in the home corner of her classroom and told her pupils about Picasso. She shared many images with them, talked about them, invited their comments and left a small group on their own to look reflectively through the books, posters and cards that she had energetically put together whilst planning this activity. She monitored their engagement with these resources from a distance and was struck by the way one five-year-old seemed particularly absorbed. The teacher recalled how the child used his fingers to trace and follow many of the lines and shapes within the drawings and paintings. Repeatedly he turned pages and slowly trailed his fingers along and around the images. After a long time, he placed the books he had been using back in the book box and went directly and without instruction to the drawing table. There he worked with complete conviction and focus until he had made a vibrant, large scale pastel drawing of a head *(see Figure C1(a) and C1(b) on page 97 in the colour section).*

This five-year-old was not capable of articulating what it was he had specifically gained from looking at the Picasso images, but what he did do was use the images at a level and in a manner which was relevant to him. He was undoubtedly intrigued by what he saw and took what he wanted from the experience. The teacher had provided the opportunity, had made sure appropriate good-quality materials, time and space were immediately available to him and had offered warm praise and encouragement. What the child did was loot Picasso's imagery in a totally natural and uncomplicated way and turned an external stimulus into something he owned.

I met this little boy two months after he had finished the drawing and was amazed at the involvement he still felt with this particular picture. I asked him if he could remember doing it and if he had looked at any artist's work at the time. He looked at me with complete scorn and said:

Yes, Picasso, Hockney and another man . . . I like my green eyes and square face . . . I was the only one who did a square face . . . I like staggery faces . . . (I'm going swimming tonight) . . . I like the colour *[he began working into the picture again]* because I've left some spaces.

We then sat on the carpet and he very determinedly searched through a huge book on Picasso and one on Van Gogh ('the other man') until he found two images which he wanted to show me 'because they are my best'. Afterwards I spoke to his mother, who was surprised to hear about our conversation.

... I didn't know he liked looking at pictures so much. An uncle frequently draws alongside him, which he likes a lot, but I didn't realise he would enjoy looking at art books, perhaps I should buy him one for Christmas. I had no idea he knew who Hockney is ... I claim no credit, his teacher is wonderful at showing them things. I do know his picture was important to him, because it is one of the few things he has come home and told us about since he started school.

USING THE WORKS OF OTHERS

Looking at art, craft and design work can often direct our way of seeing, and by sharing the outcomes of other people's visions we can become more aware of our own world. Artists/designers often represent us with the familiar, and as we focus through their eyes, we look at something afresh. The pleasure gained from this can be enormous and lasting. Apples piled high in a fruit bowl are never quite the same again if you have studied a Cézanne still life. A horse standing in a particular way becomes a frozen Elizabeth Frink sculpture. A ludicrous aggressive cockerel in a farmyard is Picasso's drawing strutting towards you. The following illustrates just how simply this can happen.

During a field trip to a local conservation centre, a teacher was sitting by a tree-lined pond overgrown with plants, lilies and weeds having a packed lunch with her class of nine-year-olds. The pupils had just completed a nature trail, when suddenly one child yelled across to her ... 'Bet Monet would like it here, Miss ...' It had been six months since the class had used Monet as a focus in their art, and the child who made the remark rarely offered comment in class. The casual observation was the only verbal evidence the teacher received that something had connected with the pupil, and it was all the more surprising (and welcome!) since the day's activities were non-art related, and it was the child who made a personal link, unprompted by her.

That children can become sensitised to their surroundings and are able to safely explore their emotions through the art and design of others I have no doubt. Their work and their conversations witness this effect time and again. But there is concern about which we should all be aware. In contemplating adult work of substance, children can certainly be helped to appreciate excellence in a range of disciplines. All but the very youngest can identify the care, commitment and sheer hard work inherent in the work of others and can often relate these qualities back to their own working methods. What pupils must never be made to feel, however, is that their own work is in any shape or form an inferior version of that which they are viewing or handling. This is a substantial issue, and care must be taken to always ensure that children's art is respected and valued on its own terms and not compared to adult pieces in a manner that de-skills or demotivates the child.

Understanding working processes

When looking at sequences of work or artists', craftworkers' and designers' sketchbooks, it is vauluble for children to see how their work developed. It also has the advantage of validating the way in which we suggest they work! I have found it useful to emphasise to pupils that professional practitioners work and re-work their ideas, that they are rarely satisfied, and that often the same subject matter or problem is dealt with repeatedly, sometimes throughout the course of a lifetime! This whole area of experience is very relevant to the child's own use of a sketchbook as a resource tool and will be referred to again later in the section about a museum visit on page 55. (See also Gillian Robinson's book *Sketchbooks: Explore and Store,* Hodder and Stoughton, 1995.)

These insights can be immensely reassuring to children and are often not talked about enough. Too often pupils have the impression that 'some clever people can just do it', which is of no comfort to them, particularly when they reach the developmental stage where

Figure 3(a)

Figure 3(b)

Figure 3(d)

Figure 3(c)

Figure 3(e)

Figures 3(a)–(e)   Eight- and nine-year-old pupils explore the work of Modigliani in their sketchbooks. The marks alongside their images show experimentation in pencil, paint and pastel as they try to determine how Modigliani might have achieved particular qualities of line and colour

27

they become highly self-critical and self-conscious and will readily judge most of their own efforts to be woefully inadequate.

The creative process is, after all, one of exploration and experimentation, of being unsure and of trying out numerous possible solutions to a problem encountered. Other curriculum areas ask pupils to draft and re-draft as they work towards a final piece, and art and design is no different. This said, I would also always defend the place of the 'one-off' spontaneous response! Sometimes a visual statement is made that is so instinctively right that to ask for it to be modified would be totally insensitive and destructive. This is as true for the professional as it is for the child in the classroom.

How pupils benefit from understanding how artists and designers work, how they can gain from encompassing artists' working methods and how they can re-use the techniques and processes of professionals in their own way and at their own level, will be returned to later. In the meantime, it is exciting to consider how ideas and influences emerge through exploring other people's art and design forms and their cultures, both past and present.

I have long believed that artists, designers and craftworkers are a band of happy, shameless thieves! They gather ideas and stimuli from all over the place – galleries, the built environment, commercial graphics, museums, foreign travel, photographs, postcards, films – the list is almost endless. Of course, artists work from their own unique imaginations, observations and memories, but all practitioners working in the visual arts will readily acknowledge influences, both contemporary and from the past, which have helped shape their work. Creativity does not happen in a vacuum, and as Hermann Leicht states in *The History of the World's Art*:

> ... art and its forms are borne upon a succession of recurring waves, and ... new forms of life and art are always the product of fresh contacts between peoples ... (Leicht, 1963)

The act of looking and of noticing the work of others might trigger a range of responses in the professional artist. A fashion designer can get excited by the dress of nomadic tribespeople and integrate observed details and colour combinations into his or her own fashion collection. A figurative painter can see the human form being dealt with from an unfamiliar point of view and wish to modify his or her own work as a result of this encounter. The skills and technical processes of others can open up new avenues of research; for example, large African coil pots can prompt the desire in a European potter to work on a totally different scale. The raku tradition of the Japanese can cause Western potters to fire their work using a newly borrowed method, whilst the study of Elizabethan miniature paintings can open up new worlds of detail and show the potential of small images.

In other words, how artists, designers and craftworkers manifest the various 'outside' influences in their own work is totally diverse in nature. The past and the present are raided to help them discover and extend their potential, but just how they do this is important. There is a vast difference between looking, researching and assimilating influences and thoughtlessly copying images for no real reason.

It would seem logical that children need to understand the difference and that the former is a thoroughly respectable and common way of working, and that they too can look anywhere, and everywhere, for ideas and possibilities to support the development of their own imagery. Civilisation might usefully be reviewed as a giant tub from which we all have permission to pluck personally defined treasure, and children need the opportunity to raid and plunder no less than the professional adult.

For me this is one of the most powerful reasons why children need access to the work of adult artists. Through knowledge, they can have it confirmed that anything and everything is possible. To know that art can work on any scale, in two or three dimensions, express emotion, question the status quo, take risks, solve problems and is only limited by the extent of the individual imagination, allows all possibilities to become theirs. To perceive that making and doing is part of the adult work can sanction creativity, lead by example and release potential in children of all ages.

2 The value of original works of art

If one is to learn to truly appreciate art and gain the most from it, nothing quite beats actually encountering the 'real' thing. To stand in front of a large vibrant canvas, to look up at the huge vaulted ceiling of a fine cathedral, to hold a delicate piece of porcelain or peer unbelievingly at an exquisite miniature have to be listed among the joys of life. The brush strokes, the marks of the chisel, the paper-thin glazed surface, each tell the story of the making, and spell out the human endeavour and commitment that have made these things come into being. Such feelings of pleasure and admiration are not only invoked in the presence of 'high art' however. The elegance of a finely crafted toy, a well-designed kitchen utensil or a beautifully tailored garment can equally afford lasting pleasure.

Wherever and whenever possible, we should plan to give children first-hand experiences. Reproductions, on paper, celluloid or the television screen, whilst being valuable can never match holding, touching and seeing originals. Of course, time, money and the pressures of delivering the whole curriculum can work against us, but if we, as teachers, don't make such encounters happen for children, then all too frequently nobody else will.

SOURCES OF ART AND ARTEFACTS

Galleries and museums are obvious places of interest and have wonderful and diverse treasures for teachers and pupils to use. The list below identifies some other less obvious but equally relevant venues for visits.

- national and local museums, galleries, exhibitions (both permanent and temporary), sculpture parks and specialist collections (for some, these are a local resource);
- local artists' studios, colleges of art and upper school art departments;
- local architecture, past and present;

- ancient sites, archives and record offices;
- appropriate local businesses such as printers, graphic design studios, architects, stonemasons and textile works.

MUSEUMS AND GALLERIES

Since the main reason for visiting such establishments is for pupils to see for themselves original works of art, craft and design, energy should be directed into ensuring that this is as rewarding and enjoyable an experience as possible.

Emphasise the need for children to take time to look closely and to respond personally, thoughtfully and questioningly. There can be few more depressing sights than young children racing around with clipboards and worksheets competing to finish first whilst they flash past amazing images and objects without a backward glance! Time, as Gombrich observed, is needed to journey into a picture.

Prior to the visit, talk through with the pupils what it is they are going to see. Build up their sense of curiosity and anticipation. Help to prepare their looking – offer focus and direction and clarify any tasks, recordings or investigations that you expect them to make *in situ*. Use sketchbooks and workbooks, and if the pupils instinctively write rather than draw, encourage them to annotate drawings, jotting down reactions, feelings and questions for consideration later, as well as making sketches and studies from the collections. Time spent with just one or two pictures or objects after a brief walk around a gallery can often prove far more valuable than trying to look at everything.

One successful 'slowing down' strategy I have adopted is to take a camera (having checked in advance that the taking of photographs is allowed), not for personal use, but so that every child can take one photograph. One film per thirty-six children is manageable financially and virtually all children are sensible when given the responsibility of using the school's or teacher's own camera. It is a device which prompts pupils to consider carefully, especially when they know that they can only take one image. I have varied the criterion for choosing the image depending on the context of the visit, but they have included the challenge to photograph:

- something you would most like to own;
- something you think you would like to have made yourself;
- something that you don't understand;
- something that has surprised you;
- something you think is really beautiful.

If you feel that the children are too young to take photographs themselves, you can always suggest they choose one for you to take on their behalf. I always have a spare register available to keep a record of what was taken and for whom – children are great at convincing you that they have been missed out! Later such class collections can become the starting points for further work, with the added bonus that the work is child selected and led.

A good talk by the gallery/museum education officer is worth its weight in gold, but an inappropriate one does more harm than good. Try to find out in advance if the person concerned is used to talking to primary-aged children and that he or she has a lively approach. Museum and gallery staff are usually more than willing to tailor your visit to your specific need and will happily prepare suitable introductions to collections/selected images, providing you give them enough warning. Thought-provoking 'children's gallery trails' are increasingly available, as are imaginative worksheets and teacher resource packs (again good for use at the planning stage).

It is welcome news when galleries and museums have 'hands on' collections. Through these, children can look and sometimes handle things at close quarters and be asked such questions as:

- What do you think this is made from?
- What does it feel like?
- What tools were used? How do you know?
- What techniques or processes were used? What are the clues?

In these circumstances, pupils have a realistic chance of becoming the visual detectives that we would like them to be. It is even better when a whole display can be touched or when art materials can be taken into display spaces for children to use whilst working in front of the pieces of their choice.

Clipboards and pencils are traditionally considered acceptable and there are many excellent crayons including watercolour pencils which extend the range of possibilities. It is exciting, however, to see that many establishments are becoming brave enough to sanction and/or instigate workshops where paint/collage materials and a range of graphic media are used in the presence of the work. A friend always includes a sandwich bag full of clay in each pupil's 'visit kit' so that they have the option to work three-dimensionally as well as two-dimensionally. She claims that it has never caused a problem, providing she remembers to pack a polythene-lined cardboard box filled with old carrier bags to protect the work and to keep it damp during the return journey.

Recently a teacher went to a major Lucien Freud exhibition at the Whitechapel Art Gallery in London and experienced the power of art to inspire new art first-hand.

> **Everywhere you turned, people were drawing, cutting, tearing and gluing – youngsters and grown-ups alike – it was brilliant!**

As in libraries, the culture within museums and art galleries has changed and is changing further. This is to be loudly applauded and if it is not the case in your region, then it is always worth raising awareness and explaining school curriculum needs in order to try to improve the facilities and benefits for your pupils.

A visit to Bury St Edmunds Art Gallery

The following is an account of a visit to Bury St Edmunds Art Gallery by a teacher and her class of ten- and eleven-year-old pupils. It illustrates the benefits of a 'good' visit, where children are able to capitalise on all that is desirable about such an occasion. The work was contemporary and the size and scale was immensely varied; the surface qualities of the pieces of sculpture were fascinating, and the whole exhibition was full of energy and surprises.

. . . A sense of excitement and anticipation preceded the visit to Bury St Edmunds Art Gallery – whether because of the specific occasion or the fact that any extra-mural activity provokes a degree of euphoria was unclear!

'Within Reach' – an exhibition of sculpture, collage and paintings (with 'viewing' facilities for the blind) – was an ideal way to introduce the children to 'real, live art' and to help them realise the role of art in the 'outside' world – several discussed the prices!

Their reaction to the display and the fact that they could actually touch and feel the exhibits was guarded. Several asked the question 'Are you sure?', and one child wanted to be reassured that he wouldn't be told off! After initial hesitation they became positively enthusiastic. Both children and teacher spent an hour and a half at the gallery, looking at the exhibition as a whole and then focusing on the work of Sophie Ryder. The children spent most of the time working on their own paper collages, referencing directly from the sculptures. Some also sketched other exhibits. *(See Figures 4(a), (b), (c) and (d) and Figures C2(a), C2(b), C2(c) and C2(d) on page 98 in the colour section.)*

The success of the trip was emphasised back at school, where the enthusiasm of the children to finish their collages and develop them into large papier-mâché sculptures was a pleasure to see. Certainly the pupils involved in this visit gained enormously from the experience. Prior to going, they had been involved in a sequence of colour work, and the teacher used some of the outcomes of these activities as preparation for the trip. The pupils had worked in 'colour families' and had experimented with painting from light to dark on a range of white and toned papers – tissue, sugar, cartridge and kitchen paper. Each child was therefore able to enter the gallery with a small folder of pre-prepared papers suitable for the planned collage making.

Figure 4(a)

Figure 4(b)

Figure 4(c)

Figure 4(d)

Figures 4(a)–(d)   Ten- and eleven-year-old pupils work directly from Sophie Ryder's sculptures and collages

Sophie Ryder produces collages as preliminary studies for her sculpture, and the children echoed this working process in reverse, that is, they studied her collages but were then invited to develop their own images by looking closely at her sculptural pieces. All the time the teacher moved from one pupil to another – praising, encouraging, asking questions. She particularly asked the pupils to work with torn rather than cut pieces and spent time pointing out the qualities of the soft edges of the various papers and showed how the tonal range available could best be exploited when recording from an original stimulus that has weight, volume and mass.

The cycle was complete when, on returning to school, the pupils used their own collages as the starting point for large-scale papier-mâché constructions, just as the artist they had studied might have done. The pupil enthusiasm, noted by the teacher, was impressive and involved large numbers of children returning voluntarily to the art area to complete their sculptures during a number of lunchtimes.

It was important that the pupils used their collages as sources of information for their sculpture making. Some pupils were pleased at how helpful theirs were to them, whilst others regretted that they had not carried out the collages from varying viewpoints in order to check specific shapes and angles. This, in turn helped the pupils to become realistic judges of their own investigative studies and automatically set the criteria for future success. They had known in advance that they were later going to need to refer to their paper pieces to help with their construction work and could therefore decide if their studies fulfilled this purpose.

This is a fundamental point to bear in mind. When pupils know what is being asked of them and they understand the parameters of a piece of work, then they are in a position to know if it has worked or not. If there are specific criteria underpinning any activity, they should be shared with the pupils at the outset – it makes no sense to hide them only to reveal them later!

ARTISTS IN RESIDENCE AND SCHOOL-BASED WORKSHOPS

One of the finest experiences for children is the opportunity to work alongside practising artists, craftworkers and designers. Through such encounters, children can witness first-hand adults and older students at work and can see materials, processes and techniques being handled in a professional manner. Residences help children of all ages to understand that art and design is something which happens in the outside world and that it is the way many different kinds of people choose to earn a living. There are many types of residencies and workshops that can be set up in a wide variety of ways. Those listed below are all worth considering.

A formal residency

Formal residencies often follow a set pattern similar to the one outlined below.

- Planning time – artist(s) and teachers plan together.
- A number of days are spent with artist(s) working in school, (either on consecutive days or staged) with pupils.
- A preliminary evaluation session is held, again with artist(s) and teachers working together.
- A written report is undertaken formally documenting the project, which may include artist, pupil and teacher evaluations, reflections on the organisation, financial and time implications (reality versus planned) and the impact on pupils' work and attitudes.

However, even within this type of formal residency which is just one of many schemes, there are variations. An alternative might take the following form:

- Artists/designers can work on their own pieces with the pupils mirroring the working process and using similar or even identical materials alongside the professional.
- Or a group project can be worked on with pupils and artist(s) evolving a piece together (see the section on A Diwali Ceremonial Project on page 50).

It is not unusual when designers or artists work on a piece mirrored by the pupils, for the work produced to be purchased by the school. Although there is no compulsion to do this, it is a way of providing the school with a tangible, long-term legacy of the residency, which in turn becomes an original image or artefact to which future generations of pupils can refer.

A formal residency of this sort can often be co-funded by the school and other appropriate bodies, most notably the Regional Arts Boards. It is necessary to contact such a body well in advance of hoped-for funding in order to find out application details and procedures and to see if priority has been assigned to certain categories of work or specific practitioners (for example, environmental installations, black artists, group work, integrated arts projects, etc).

Some people seem to believe that this kind of residency is only available and applicable to the secondary sector. This is not the case; the primary sector is equally eligible to apply for Regional Arts funding, and many schools have benefited from successful applications.

A hands-on day

This can be an occasion when your school discovers who its real friends are.

Some primary schools are beginning to develop a network of local art, craft and design workers who are prepared to give up one day (perhaps just once a year) to come and work in school. On page 50, I describe a specific instance in a first school where a large group of practitioners came together and spent a day working in the school hall. It was the second time that the school had organised such an event, and plans are well ahead for the third, with a commitment to making it an annual event.

Such days do, by definition, only allow for 'taster' sessions but are nonetheless valuable. Indeed, for young children whose concentration spans are often short, they can be particularly appropriate encounters. They allow for friendly conversations and the asking of questions on territory familiar to the child, and can do much to stimulate curiosity and pupil interest.

These occasions also reinforce pupil understanding of the diverse nature of art, craft and design and can become celebrations of local skills and expertise. Indeed, anything that helps to show that such people work in and around the community is a healthy realisation for all youngsters to have and underlines the fact that making and doing are not always inaccessible activities carried out by remote individuals in distant places.

Art weeks

Increasingly it seems that primary schools are using art weeks as a device for focusing on the visual and other art forms (dance, drama, music). This approach is sometimes thematic in nature when, for example, an environmental theme or a recycling project provides the link for the endeavours. Recently I have worked with colleagues under the broad titles of 'Celebrations', 'Inside/Outside' and 'Metamorphosis' and all proved exciting starting points from which many ideas developed. Other schools with which I have been involved have wanted such weeks to be process-led and as a result have opted for a textile week (see Figures C25(a), C25(b), C25(c) and C25(d) on page 120), a printmaking week or a week of working three-dimensionally. The choice has been made after the whole staff group has identified a curriculum area that they wish to develop or feel they have allocated too little time or attention to in the past. The logistics of such a week can be quite daunting to organise, and planning, as ever, needs to be thorough. But with energy and determination they can be highly successful and beneficial to both staff and pupils.

Figure 5   A class of eight-year-olds show off their results of an art week, focusing on working with textiles

Listed below are some key questions to consider when planning for the smooth running of an art week:

- Is there enough specialist support available (artists, craftworkers, relevant advisory teachers, art students)?
- Will the whole school be able to come off its usual timetable for the entire week or just each afternoon or other specified part of the day?
- Will the school stay on its timetable with each class or year group being rotated into specific activities?
- Will a visit to an appropriate gallery or exhibition be built into the week?
- Will sufficient funding be allocated for materials, and will such materials be centrally held or assigned to a number of work stations? (Fairness of access and amounts of materials available to each working group can often make or break these initiatives, particularly by the end of the week!)
- Will there be opportunities for parental and older pupil (GCSE and A level) involvement?
- Will the week culminate in an exhibition or open day, or is this best done two or three weeks later?
- Will staff be able to be released in rotation so that the week can act as an in-house Inset for individual teachers, thereby enhancing long-term benefits to the school?

An informal residency

These residencies are more generally used in secondary schools, but could be equally valuable in the primary sector. The idea is that the school offers a working space, at no cost, to an artist or craftsperson, either for an agreed time span or on an open-ended basis. The artist expects to be self-sufficient in terms of providing his or her own materials and equipment and anticipates no payment for being in school. He or she must, of course, agree to visits by pupils and teachers and to become part, in a strictly non-teaching capacity, of the school community.

Some schools have little space to spare and may therefore find it very difficult to explore this kind of possibility. There are, however, establishments that have space in excess of requirements, (or have a particularly large entrance or other communal area) which could be used as a mini-workshop or studio space. The one thing that many young artists and designers do not have and cannot afford, particularly when first out of art college, is space (and warmth!). Ideas and the desire to continue to work in their chosen area exist in full measure, but money for establishing their own workspace is difficult to find. Schools in turn can find it difficult to fund more than the very occasional residency, but this arrangement of 'adopting' an aspiring artist can allow for ongoing contact with a practitioner in a supportive, enlightening and formative manner.

Two secondary schools I know have been even more imaginative in exploiting the possibilities of this idea and now pay two artists (in these cases a painter and a potter) to be technicians for two days a week. For the remaining three days, the artists practise their own crafts. Primary schools could possibly utilise such individuals in an ancillary or lunchtime-assistant capacity in a similar manner.

This kind of informal agreement can work brilliantly, particularly if the artist chosen creates a studio-type environment which shows resources, referencing materials, sketchbooks and working drawings being used. In the two schools mentioned above, the pupils have developed immense loyalty to 'their' artists and talk knowledgeably about the work they see being produced.

Do's and don'ts applicable to any kind of residency or workshop

- The importance of planning residencies and workshops thoroughly cannot be overstated, and it is essential that you allow enough time for discussion and for agreements to be reached. The only times I have witnessed residencies get into difficulties are when there has been a mismatch of expectations and understanding by the parties concerned.
- As far as possible, enable the whole staff to be involved from the planning stage through to implementation and final

evaluation. At the very least, keep all colleagues informed and as a matter of courtesy introduce the artist(s) to everyone, including all the pupils. Even if pupils are not going to be involved directly, five minutes of assembly time spent welcoming the visitor(s) and launching a project is time well spent. Include parents by inviting them in to see what is happening and arrange time after school for them to meet the artist. These may sound like very basic points, and indeed they are, but it is alarming how many times I have either seen or taken part in really dynamic and exciting work at one end of a school only to discover that only a tiny percentage of the school population knows anything about it. This is obviously a missed opportunity.

- Agree any funding or payments and deliver such monies on time. The artist may happily accept reimbursement for money spent on consumables but may prefer to provide the school with a list of requirements (adhering to an agreed set budget) for the school to order. Delivery time would therefore need to be allowed for.
- Be realistic about the number of pupils that can work with an artist at any one time and do not try and squeeze in too many.
- Choose your artist(s) with care. People with the right personality who relate well with children and who produce work of quality are obviously your ideal candidates. Help and advice in locating such individuals is available through a number of sources: local education authority art and design advisers, inspectors and advisory teachers will be able to direct you. So too will the Regional Arts Boards, who keep directories of approved practitioners and slide libraries of their work to help you in your selection process. Other outside agencies, such as The Arts Education for a Multicultural Society (AEMS), are worth trying. The AEMS project has been set up to promote the use of black and Asian artists in all sectors of the education system and they have a directory which includes approved visual artists

willing to work in schools. The SHAPE/Artlink Network also provides a link service between artists of every discipline and creatively deprived sectors of the community (including children with special needs through physical or mental handicap). This is a national network with regional offices located throughout the country. Lastly, ask for personal recommendations from local or regional art colleges and universities with art and design departments, concerning current or ex-students who would be willing to undertake projects or work within your school.

However, it is not always necessary to visit a museum or gallery or arrange residencies in order for pupils to see and touch original works of art and design. There are other strategies at our disposal, some of which are discussed below.

LOCAL EDUCATION AUTHORITY AND/OR MUSEUM LOAN SCHEMES

Many local education authorities and museums have loan schemes available for use in schools. The length of time that images and objects are allowed to stay in a school may vary, but both kinds of scheme are there to encourage hands-on experiences for pupils. Once again, planning is demanded, as it is necessary for teachers to familiarise themselves with what is available locally and regionally and for required items or collections to be booked well in advance of planned use. The range available from museums may include:

- stuffed birds, reptiles, butterflies and animals;
- fossils and bones – including complete skeletons, skulls and shells;
- eggs and nests and other habitats, including wasp nests and bee honeycombs;
- artefacts and design forms from different times and places, for example, Anglo-Saxon pots and jugs, medieval shoes, North American Indian beadwork, lengths of textile work from different geographical locations and Indian printing blocks.

Obviously these items present themselves as ideal subject matter for direct observational drawing, but the sensitive teacher can extend their potential and use them to form interesting links with original works of art and design. For instance, a medieval shoe can be the start of a 'shoe hunt' – What are the children wearing in a Brueghel painting? What are monks wearing in illustrated manuscripts? What do the characters in the Bayeaux tapestry or in an Egyptian wall painting have on their feet? This is fun, but the serious value of the exercise is in encouraging children to observe closely.

Likewise, a stuffed cockerel can lead on to looking at paintings, prints and drawings executed by such artists as Picasso or Michael Rothenstein. A child's drawing of a stuffed hare can be used in relation to Albrecht Dürer's famous study of the same creature. A bee honeycomb can be compared with and contrasted to the book illustration by Kit Williams, and drawings of birds and butterflies can be explored through referencing the drawings of scientific explorers who first recorded species on early voyages of discovery.

Local education authority original works of art collections vary in nature and size; some have extensive collections, whilst others have none. Some have bought the work of regional artists and craftworkers and are contemporary in feel, whilst others have come about through individual bequests and donations and are more haphazard in nature. Teachers will need to ask what is available and find out if there exists any support or background information, or teaching packs that have been developed to help primary teachers use such collections effectively.

A few local authorities have encouraged the setting up of specific display sites in schools, ideally complete with good-quality display boards, adjustable shelving systems and spotlights located on ceiling tracking. Such schools can receive a set number of works of art and design on a rotational basis, usually once a term. This idea of 'art on the move' travelling exhibitions can be very successful, especially when teachers have the opportunity to know well in advance what is coming to them next, and teacher Inset sessions are organised for colleagues to share how they might use such resources. However, it is a great shame that funding for many such schemes has now either ceased or is in jeopardy through education 'reforms', local education authority reorganisations and the closing of professional development and/or teacher's centres, which often acted as the administrative base for such schemes.

Some individual schools have a policy for purchasing both original works of art and design and good-quality reproductions. In some areas, groups of schools have chosen to cluster together to swap and share originals to everyone's benefit. Positive relationships with local artists, designers and craftworkers, perhaps fostered through such occasions as a 'hands-on day' such as the one described earlier, may well lead to these people being willing to lend schools their work on a short- or long-term basis – it is always worth asking!

THE USE OF SECONDARY SOURCE MATERIAL

Life is interesting when we feed off a mixed and varied diet, both literally and metaphorically, and this is equally true when it comes to using resources in the classroom. Children can only benefit from having access to as many resources as possible, from as wide a range as possible, to include books, posters, large reproductions, postcards, slides and videos, as well as artefacts and aesthetic, decorative and functional designed forms.

The above resources, known as secondary resource materials, have both advantages and disadvantages, and it is useful to think these through. All resources vary in quality and all can mislead. For instance, bear in mind that the size of an image projected on a screen can become much larger than the original and a paper-based reproduction is much smaller. Pupil's understanding of the original can, therefore, be easily distorted. The accuracy of colour reproduction is immensely variable, and pupils can often gain little sense of the true colour values of the real thing. The surface qualities and textural nature of many artefacts are also rarely captured in a photograph.

However, there are two strategies which can help to counteract these problems. Whenever possible, cut a piece of paper to the exact size of the original so that any discrepancy will be made clear. If the original is a huge canvas or mural, I have had children pace out the dimensions and we have all held hands to enclose the space taken up by the image. 'Wow, can a picture really be this big, Miss?' is a frequent response!

Now and again, take photographs of the children's own work and compare and contrast them with their originals. This activity can elicit a range of responses such as: 'It looks much better smaller', 'It doesn't look nearly so interesting', 'The colours are all wrong' or 'But ours aren't all the same size'. This can certainly help younger pupils to understand that what they see in books is not 'it' but a visual record of something quite different.

A teacher was working with a class on landscape imagery and showed the pupils some of Constable's paintings in the form of postcards. She asked many questions – What time of day is it? What time of year? What was the weather like? How can we find out the answers to these questions? What are the clues? – when an earnest eight-year-old said, 'I think Constable must have taken this one in the afternoon because of where the sun is'. It was only at this point that the teacher realised that the little girl thought that she was looking at a set of Constable's photographs, no different from her own family snapshots. The teacher subsequently took a photograph of one of the little girl's paintings, talked to her about the two images and was able to reassure herself that greater understanding had taken place.

ADVANTAGES OF RESOURCE MATERIALS

In this next section I have grouped various resource materials into categories in order to look at their advantages when used in the classroom. Hopefully it will help teachers to analyse what they want to achieve and how they can best accomplish this using the available resources.

Advantages of slides

One of the main advantages of using slides is that the whole class can respond to a single image, and the teacher can question, make comment and direct the attention of the class simultaneously. If a slide projector is used, it can also help some pupils to speak in the quasi-anonymity of a darkened room. Alternatively individuals or small groups can use slides with hand-held viewers, or large table top light boxes.

Many galleries, museums and commercial companies sell slides of excellent quality covering many different subjects, which means a teacher can slowly build up his or her own set of slides tailored to planned work, such as details of local buildings of architectural interest, etc. They are also an excellent way of preparing pupils for a gallery/museum visit and/or for use in follow-up work.

Advantages of reproductions: postcards, posters, etc.

The advantages of the different kinds of reproductions are many. They are readily obtainable and available for all to handle. They enable pupils to choose their own imagery from which to work or make reference and are ideal for small group or paired work. They are excellent for the purposes of comparison and contrast, and in the case of posters and other large images, often make apparent individual brush strokes and other mark-making techniques. Postcard-sized reproductions can be grouped into sets by teachers and pupils to aid thematic and project work and stored in boxfiles or manilla folders. Added to this, pupils can probably afford to collect postcards and reproductions of artwork from magazines to place and use in sketchbooks, and indeed, as many newspaper and magazine cuttings can be deemed expendable, any special images from them could be laminated and thus made more durable. Finally, reproductions of all sizes and shapes are easy to use for display purposes.

Advantages of books

It is important for teachers to consider the inclusion of books with good reproductions as an integral part of the school or classroom library. It is also useful to consider story books with interesting illustrations – of which there are many, often containing different techniques such as drawings, pen and inkwork, paintings and collage.

Books can be used either individually or in groups. The range, quality and content available is immense and can therefore expose pupils to many art, craft and design practitioners from all over the world, both past and present, and can help pupils to understand that the making of art is considerable, widespread and ongoing in the adult world. Books can provide teachers and pupils with biographical and anecdotal information about artists, images and artefacts, as well as helping teachers to strengthen their pupils' knowledge of any conceptual areas difficult to cover in their own geographical location and to ensure breadth of coverage, for example, sculpture, work of women artists, textile and fashion design, etc. School library services are often able to provide 'book boxes' in support of themes/topics/ specific subject matter, and it is always worth considering cutting up some cheap books to use the plates as single reproductions.

Advantages of video and film

Videos and film provide an excellent medium for pupils to watch artists, craftworkers and designers at work. In some cases, it may even be possible for teachers to make their own videos where space and time make a whole-class visit impracticable. It will be up to the individual teacher to approach the artist/designer concerned. Schools television art programmes increasingly take account of the need for pupils to witness artists at work, and good-quality recordings are available which are aimed specifically at the primary age group and which reflect the breadth and range of the visual art world.

Advantages of artefacts and ephemera

By artefacts and ephemera I mean collections, such as those listed below. However, obviously these are only suggestions – new categories can be devised and the lists of possibilities within each are almost endless. Go with your own enthusiasms and interests and those of your colleagues and the children.

- *Functional objects*: jugs, teapots, clocks, spoons, keys, button boxes (decorative and functional), salt cellars, candlesticks, purses, washbags, brushes for different purposes, beach toys and bath toys.
- *Fashion and textiles*: shoes, jewellery, lengths of fabrics of different kinds and from different countries (raid market stalls and remnant boxes), hats, handbags/evening bags, scarves, pillow cases and cushions. (See Figures C3(a), C3(b), C3(c) and C3(d) on page 99 in the colour section.)
- *Graphic design*: carrier bags, invitations, product boxes, tape, CD and video covers (including ones that relate to pupils' own age group), book jackets, tickets and price tags, and empty matchboxes.

The advantages of using such items are that they are readily available, often at little or no cost, and can come from the children's own worlds (home, school, shops, holidays). Parents and extended families can be asked to participate in building up collections. Because of their nature, most will be available for all to handle, and they are ideal for activities which involve comparing and contrasting and for confirming that there is more than one solution to any design problem. They help to illustrate the range of craft and design work in the *real* world and can be used simultaneously to cover many curriculum areas (especially design and technology, humanities and science). Displayed collections will enrich the learning environment, and many become wonderful resources for direct observational drawing.

3 Ideas in action

In their book *Drawing to learn* (also in this series), Dawn and Fred Sedgwick remind us of the value of surprising children. To offer the unexpected, to challenge preconceptions and reveal new possibilities are indeed powerful ways of extending creative horizons. But perhaps adults need jolts and surprises every bit as much as the pupils.

Who said, for instance, that art should be rectangular and permanent? Absolutely no one, and yet we can find ourselves repeatedly offering small white rectangular paper surfaces to children as though they are the only prerequisites for image making. Children find it great fun to work on great sheets of torn brown paper, or long thin till rolls begged from the nearest supermarket, or on panels of rough plywood taken from discarded orange boxes at the end of market day. Think how compelling it is to trail one's fingers through trays of flour or salt only to tap the tray in order to start over again. We have never stopped making sandcastles, even though we know for certain that the next tide will treat such forms with absolute disdain.

It is the way of artists to explore surfaces and investigate any available materials. Rough, smooth, resistant and non-resistant, porous, symmetrical and irregular – these and many other surfaces have been seized in order to explore their characteristics and to exploit particular qualities. A friend once gave me a large sheet of fine sandpaper as a Christmas gift. 'Have you not drawn on this stuff?' she enquired, 'It's wonderful, particularly for working into with pastels – the pastels bond with the surface and produce a smashing effect – try it, you can get some effects which no other materials seem to give!'

A DIWALI CEREMONIAL PROJECT

Perhaps I am more likely than some to encounter the unexpected, since one of the privileges of my job is that I am invited into large numbers of schools of different types, sectors and size. Each has the potential to surprise. (See Figures C4(a), C4(b), C4(c), and C4(d) on page 100 in the colour section.) Very recently I was asked to a special school to take part in an afternoon's Diwali ceremonial project being led by a group called 'Sharing in Art'. I knew this group to be an organisation for artists from various cultural backgrounds who combine their specialist knowledge in order to organise projects which explore the potential of shared creativity. An information handout which they produced stated: 'The group aims to set up a non-competitive environment in which individuals can interact freely, influencing each other's ideas and approaches to art and its materials.'

I didn't know much more than this, but the first hint that something exciting was going on was when a young pupil burst through the front door I was approaching, grinning from ear to ear and with huge red and orange smudges across her face and upwards from finger tips to elbows. 'We are doing art,' she laughed, 'I think I have to wash now.'

On walking the length of a short corridor, I was hit by a breathtaking sight as I turned into the school hall. The entire hall floor, some 20 × 8 metres in size, was being used as a vast canvas by sixty special needs children and their teachers. Dillip Sur, one of the artists involved, had introduced the meaning of Diwali by speaking about how it was celebrated in India. He shared photographs and descriptions with the pupils, who had previously done a lot of work on the cultures and traditions of Indian society. The pupils, their teachers and the 'Sharing in Art' group had then begun to work together to create a huge decorative floor piece (see page 52).

To begin with, the pupils were asked to explore the school grounds for natural materials:

Find the most colourful leaves, select the prettiest pebbles, collect pots of earth and sand from the play area – are there any patterned bits of bark or twisty twigs? Search and find what you think is really beautiful and bring it back to the hall.

Once they had finished their collections, they were given bowls of colour powder pigment and Indian Rangoli pattern makers. These consist of tubes filled with powdered pigment, pierced at intervals so that when they are rolled, colour streams out to form immaculate repeat patterns. Surprise and delight registered with children and adults alike, as the piece grew and grew. The whole experience became a time of magic for everyone. A brilliant cobalt haze was sieved across red ochres; a giant green figure was outlined by carefully placed leaves; spirals, coils and whirls flowed amongst swathes of orange and purple pigments. The Rangoli pattern makers enthralled. None of us had seen them before and the instant and simple way they worked was fascinating.

For two hours the piece took shape. Once finished, everyone stood at the end of the hall (with some outside looking in through windows to get another view) to simply enjoy that which had been jointly made. No one person could have achieved such a spectacle. It lay like an intricate banner or tapestry covering every square centimetre of the floor and was a testimony to collaborative effort and energy.

Figure 6(a)   Dillip Sur from 'Sharing in Art' listens . . .

Figure 6(b)   . . . whilst an eleven-year-old girl gives her thoughts on the project

The pupils loved the immediacy of the workshop and felt proud that they had all contributed equally. They were staggered by the sheer size of their image and that their environment had been so radically altered. One of the teachers reflected:

> I just can't believe this. It has worked on so many levels. The thing itself is amazing, the children have worked as a giant team with no problems, they have made lots of decisions for themselves, they have modified and developed imagery, and we did it all in one afternoon.

It has given me so many ideas, I'm sure we could do something similar ourselves in the summer outside . . . we can't let this be just a one-off experience . . . At the moment I feel as though I never want to work on paper again!

After another two hours, the pupils went home, and the image was swept, brushed and vacuumed away. The piece could only ever have been temporary and was orchestrated by the artists to be so. But the value of the workshop and its impact on the pupils was immense. They have spoken about it at great length since and perhaps, like a vivid dream, it may live on in their minds for a long time to come.

AN ARTISTS' AND CRAFTWORKERS' DAY

One school with which I have a lot of contact has been very positive in its approach to exposing pupils to practising artists and designers, and has many ongoing strategies in place. One of these, as mentioned earlier, is an annual 'artists' and craftworkers' day'. This event has been masterminded by one particularly energetic teacher who has done much to develop the art and design curriculum in the school. She describes the day below:

All children, including the nursery, could observe and try out a variety of skills alongside the artists and craftspeople who are now thought of as friends of the school. Our guests include a lino-cut printer who showed the older children how she made a final print using different cutting marks, indicating specific points through the examples she had brought with her. During the day she worked on two large bird images using potato prints. She cut into the potato with as much accuracy as she would into lino, which provided a good contrast to the children's more usual and less considered way of printing with potatoes. She went on to show them how to use more than one colour and the children, following her working process, were totally absorbed in newly discovered possibilities.

Figure 7 Before starting his own work, a seven-year-old boy looks and listens as an adult printmaker makes a potato print

A potter from the local middle school worked with our pupils using a range of simple pushing, pinching and rolling techniques and encouraged the use of a variety of tools. He later took the pupils' work back to his own school and then delivered a fired and glazed treasure trove back to us.

A calligrapher demonstrated the wonderful control demanded by his craft and even the youngest had a go at writing their names. *(See Figures C5(a) and C5(b) on page 101 in the colour section.)*

There was a chance to try carding and spinning with a weaver, and other textilers involved in the day included a patchwork quilt maker, a knitter and a specialist in cross-stitch. One further worker showed the pupils Paul Klee images of colourful buildings, offered interesting fabrics and began to create a stitched fabric collage with the children. This went so well that she volunteered to return to the school to work with one of the classes, and so emerged another bonus of the day!

We also had a group of sixth formers from our neighbouring upper school join us, and this added another dimension. Some of these students brought large paintings already in progress and continued to work on them. They soon had children painting on big sheets of paper at their feet, simply inspired by their enthusiasm and the scale of the pieces. Another group worked with the children on a life-sized skeleton using rolled newspaper and masking tape and painting it in vivid colours. This was considered great fun and it was satisfying to see very young children and older students working together in an open and friendly way.

The teacher started working in this school with no art training and no contacts with the local art fraternity, but through her own interest and zeal she has made art and design a thriving subject. She regularly uses a local gallery, has organised museum visits and trips to the National Gallery in London and frequently attends their teacher workshop sessions. This year her successes were acknowledged when the National Gallery asked her to deliver an illustrated talk on her work with young children after they had seen some images in the style of Matisse that she produced with a class of five-year-olds (see Figures 32(a) and 32(b) on page 126).

The day described needed a reasonable amount of organisation and created extra administration, but the benefits to all pupils far outweighed these factors. The artists and craftworkers gained also – a number (there were twelve adults participating) had not known each other beforehand and enjoyed meeting up. The sixth formers have invited the pupils they worked with to their A-level exhibition at the end of the academic year, and the primary pupils are looking forward to seeing their "big friends" finished paintings.

A MUSEUM VISIT WITHIN AN INTEGRATED PROJECT

In some subject areas, the National Curriculum requires that certain topics are dealt with within specific Key Stages. For the primary sector, the National Curriculum art document is not 'content driven' in this way, and teachers can make a professional judgement as to when and how art can usefully be integrated with other curriculum areas. The history document has allowed for an integrated approach to be adopted in interesting ways, and many valuable projects have emerged that deal with links, for example, between the historical aspects of the Anglo Saxons, Vikings and Victorian Britain and the art and artefacts of these periods.

The following shows how a school uses their study of the Greeks and related artwork of this time in a mutually profitable way. Using both original and secondary source materials, this approach successfully expands the children's learning of art and history at the same time.

Initially the pupils had been learning about life in ancient Greece from many different sources, including looking at a number of books showing archaeological evidence of this civilisation. They talked about Greek theatre conventions and the construction of the amphitheatres, monumental sculpture and relief panels and their use in the decoration of buildings. The pupils looked particularly closely at pots, vases and plates in order to learn about everyday life of the period. Predictably, perhaps, they enjoyed identifying the athletes, musicians and dancers and liked the stories told through the decoration on these vessels – Theseus slaying the Minotaur was a particular favourite.

The teacher pointed out that early pots were painted in such a way that the figures were black silhouettes against red clay, but that later this was reversed so that the background was painted black and the figures were left in the natural colour of the clay. At this stage pupils selected a favourite design and made large-scale drawings (see Figures C6(a) and C6(b) on page 102 in the colour section) using books for guidance. This was not, however, a simple copying exercise. The teacher asked them to notice how and where the Greek pot-painters placed their images in relation to the size and shape of the vessel, and further asked them to find out by looking carefully what information they could gather about the clothing and fashions of the time. All this was fine preparation for a planned visit to the Fitzwilliam Museum in Cambridge and the clay work that the teacher knew was going to be carried out later.

At the museum, the children were excited to find they could identify many of the artefacts with which they had become familiar through this preliminary book-based research. They drew objects and

Figures 8(a) & (b)
Images drawn in
sketchbooks on a
museum visit by
seven- and eight-year-
olds for use later on
plate designs

images in their sketchbooks that particularly appealed to them. The
pupils knew by now that they were to become 'pot-painters' on their
return to school and had been asked to gather images that might be
used for this purpose. Some children recalled their previously
acquired 'specialist' knowledge, and one child was heard to say to
another, 'No, Miss said it was black first, then red', apparently
irritated that her friend had forgotten the sequence.

Other drawings were intended to add to their knowledge of Greek
life and the technology of the time. Drawings of furniture, lamps,
shoes, armour and jewellery became tangible evidence of their
investigations. The children knew that their time for sketching in the
museum was limited, and their drawings reflect a busy and focused
approach. They all stuck impressively to the tasks set (which included
completing other topic sheets), and it was obvious that this resulted
from the thoughtfully organised preparation work done in the
classroom prior to the visit.

Back at school, they used the information to help with other
aspects of the topic work, and from the art point of view, they created

A Greek Helmet.   A Greek Helmet.

Leg pads.   Spear.   Bow and arrows

Sheild   Sword   Club   Axe

A Greek Woman.   A Greek Man.

A Couch.   Lamps

Figures 9(a) & (b) Two eight-year-olds select Greek items which interest them

their own designs for the dishes reproduced in the colour section. (See Figure C7 on page 103 in the colour section.) Their designs resulted from their drawings in the museum and thus show a culmination of a well planned sequence of work that moved from using secondary source materials, through direct observation of original artefacts and into three-dimensional responses to knowledge gained.

USING THE ENVIRONMENT

Buildings provide a rich and readily available resource, whatever the geographical location of the school. The school building itself can be used to great effect. In the drawings that follow, young children record the building of an extension to an original Victorian structure, and both the old and the new are carefully observed. Figure 10(a) shows the protective orange fencing beyond which the pupils were not allowed to go. The boy who made this drawing decided he had shown enough of the pattern of the fencing because, 'It's all the same, isn't it?' The rivets used in the construction of the conservatory spaces built on to the ends of some of the classroom areas appear to strongly capture the imagination! The pupils had seen great numbers loaded into a 'gun' used by the workman and had been very impressed by (and envious of!) the sound and strength of this power tool – hence the importance of these shapes in the drawing (see Figure 10(b)).

Figure 10(a)
Figure 10(c)

Figure 10(b)
Figure 10(d)

Figures 10(a)–(d)   Five- and six-year-olds record
the old and the new parts of their school

The idea of old and new is a good approach to take with buildings. For instance, pupils could record patterns, making drawings of old and new roof tiles, bricks, paved areas, fences, windows and gates. Questions such as: Who made these, from what and when? can lead to discussion on the hand-crafted and the mass-produced, changes in materials used, and methods of construction in different periods.

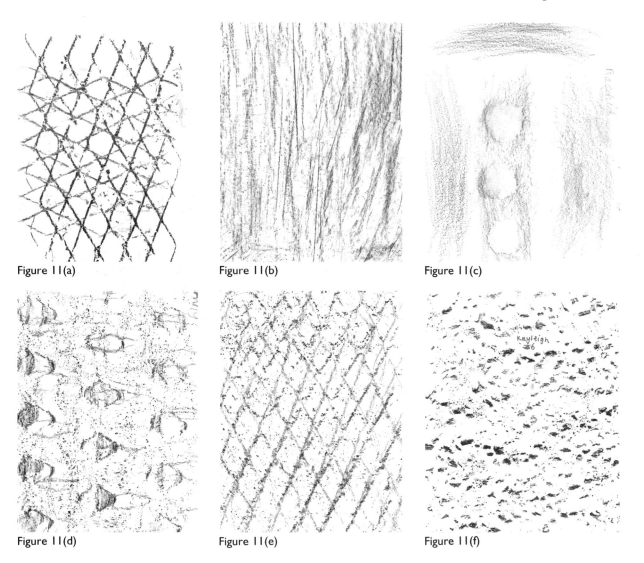

Figure 11(a)

Figure 11(b)

Figure 11(c)

Figure 11(d)

Figure 11(e)

Figure 11(f)

Figures 11(a)–(f)   The same five- and six-year-olds record surfaces by rubbing sections of the building and the materials to be used for the extension. These became evidence in their 'pattern hunt' and were later used in discussion about surfaces and textures

Interiors and exteriors can also be explored – look into, out of and through spaces and half-open doors. Compare and contrast children's findings with Dutch paintings of courtyards and room interiors and the images produced by the modern American painter, Edward Hopper, of looking through windows into rooms beyond, along with those of other contemporary artists.

Other places which relate to the children's own world can offer opportunities for design activities. Adventure playgrounds and assault courses may not be architectural jewels, but they have real significance for children and are helpful in as much as their skeletal nature makes their construction obvious. They are usually built from materials that young children can identify and relate to – wood, plastic, rope and rubber – but most importantly, they are child-size and fun.

Figures 12(a) & (b)
Children's adventure playgrounds

Figure 12(a)

Figure 12(b)

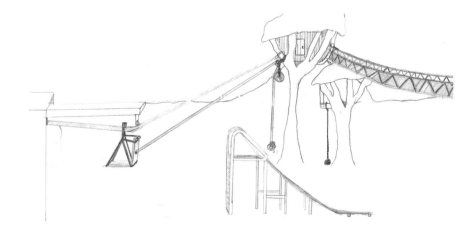

Figure 13(a)

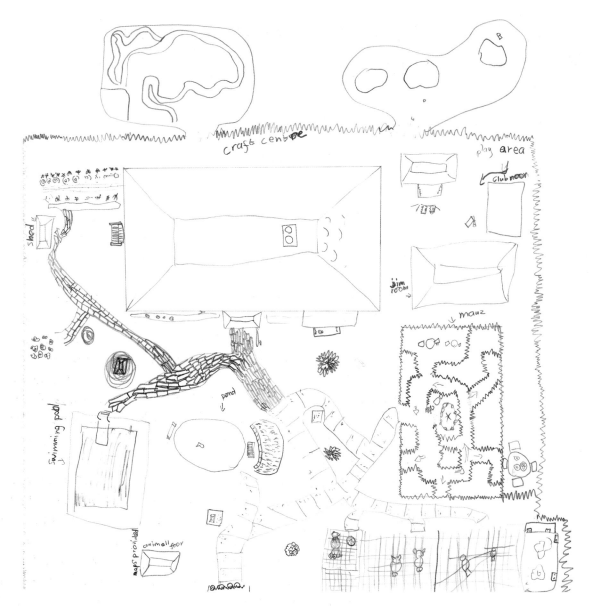

craft centre

play area

clubroom

shed

gim room

mauz

swimming pool

pond

animall foor

maps provided

Figure 13(b)

Figures 13(a) and 13(b)   show imagined play areas designed by a ten- and eleven-year-old. The children not only draw with authority, but it is clear that they are drawing from knowledge and first-hand experience

4 Timing the introduction of artefacts

USING ARTEFACTS AT THE BEGINNING OF A PROJECT

The intention behind using works of art, design and craft in the many ways considered so far is, of course, that it should be helpful to the pupils. With this in mind, careful consideration needs to be given as to exactly when a particular reference should be introduced. If original art and artefacts or secondary resources are always used as an initial stimulus and starting point for children's own work, then a number of responses may occur.

For instance, pupils rapidly make assumptions – 'We are being shown "X" and so now our teacher wants us to produce something that looks approximately like "X"' – and this in turn can result in shallow mimicry. Alternatively, this way of working becomes predictable and is perceived by the pupils to be dull; rather than being motivated by others, the pupils switch off. Added to this, pupils can find themselves unable to relate to the work being used because they have had no opportunity to make any connections with it through lead-in time.

The negative approaches outlined above can be particularly true when pupils are being asked to work from a process or technical point of view. If pupils are being shown, for example, woodcuts or linocuts and they have had no experience of relief printing methods such as card blocks, string blocks or pressprint, then it is very difficult for them to know what it is they are looking at. Of course, few things can be truly 'shared' experiences – just because pupils are unable to chisel away at a block of marble does not mean that they are unable to look at Michelangelo's sculptures – but where it is relevant and possible, pupils benefit from experiencing 'approximations' prior to looking analytically at the work of others. There is little point, for instance, in pupils being asked to respond to thickly applied paint on an artist's canvas if their only experience is of using watercolour boxes or thin powder paint. Here it would make sense for a discussion and practical exploration to take place about the quality and nature of various kinds of paints, dyes and drawing inks and for experiments to be carried out prior to encountering the pictures chosen for reference (see Figure C8 on page 104 in the colour section).

When encouraging the use of thick paint, such experiments could include mixing ready-mix paints and powder colour together and mixing powder paints with adhesives and sand or sawdust. These could then be trialled on different surfaces, for example on small bits of different kinds of paper, bits of cloth (cotton, canvas, hessian or sacking) and card off-cuts or cardboard box off-cuts. The experimental paints could then be applied to surfaces using fingers, glue spreaders and spatulas of varying sizes and bits of card or plastic.

These investigation pieces could be fixed with adhesives onto class or individual sample boards, with explanatory notes made alongside each piece. This would provide a stimulus for further discussion, whilst providing a source of reference for future projects.

It still means, of course, that pupils are not handling oil paints or expensive acrylic colours, but it will mean that they are in an informed position concerning the use of paint of a similar consistency and textural quality as the artist(s) they are studying.

USING ARTEFACTS IN THE MIDDLE OF A PROJECT

When art works are introduced during the course of a sequence or unit of work, pupils often seem to feel very positive about their own images, especially when they can identify similarities: 'I've made marks like him!' 'My colours are kind of the same.' 'Can I try to make mine more like this one now?' From the teacher's point of view, it allows such comments as: 'You have been working really well/ interestingly; would you like to see the work of someone who has worked in a similar way?' or 'I think this person has used their pencils just like you, can we see if they can give us a few more ideas so that we can develop our drawings further?' (See Figure C9 on page 104 in the colour section.)

Obviously the children's task has to be orchestrated by the teacher to make sure such 'coincidences' occur, but many colleagues have found that using the art/design work of others as a midpoint boost has brought a sense of surprise to the children's learning, and has enabled pupils to sustain their own pieces for longer than might otherwise have been the case. It also appears to reinforce the value that some pupils place on their efforts when they can see echoes of their own achievements unexpectedly appearing within the work of 'grown-ups'.

Despite the thrust of this book being concerned with using art and artefacts with children, I feel it would be a great mistake for it to be thought that we cannot sometimes say, 'Today we are just looking'. To look, with no task in mind is immensely important. At the end of a unit of work, it can be a valuable experience to reflect back with the pupils on what they have achieved and to offer images of similar intent or purpose and enjoy their outcomes, alongside the outcomes of others, with a view to getting pleasure out of both.

Figure 14(a)

Figure 14(b)

Figures 14(a) & (b) 'Today we are just talking and listening.' Here the painter Tom Phillips visits the school to talk about his work and to answer the pupils' questions. The children decide that he cannot leave until they have his autograph!

AN END IN ITSELF

The art of just looking and enjoying can often be sadly lacking in today's crowded curriculum. Art, design and craftwork can afford much quiet pleasure to the individual if only we can find time in the school week to make this possible. The following suggestions may help to create such opportunities:

1   Now and again substitute pictures, objects and/or art books in place of the going-home storytime. The end of the day can be a good time to look at and talk about pictures and objects. Two or three contrasting pictures (in style, content or place of origin) can be compared and discussed. A selection of books, postcards or slides (maybe with a subject matter link) can be looked at. Each pupil can be invited to choose a favourite picture. If over a period of time each person has a turn, eventually a 'class gallery' of individual choices can be pinned up (this is one good use of a classroom postcard collection). Occasionally, substitute asking the pupils to choose a favourite story with asking them to decide which book illustrations they like best. This can lead on to talking about how pictures and stories relate, different illustrative styles, photographs versus drawings and the diverse arrangements of page layouts.

2   Instigate 'The picture or object of the day/week/month' to be placed in a corridor, entrance area or library space. Some schools have taken this practice on board with great enthusiasm and success. The idea has become established and everyone is given the chance to take part – pupils, cooks, cleaners, governors, parents and caretakers as well as teachers. The only 'rule' is that participants are asked to write a short statement saying why they have made their selection. I recently saw a beautiful teapot that a caretaker had chosen as his favourite object. His reason for choosing the object was, 'Because it has been in my house since I was a little boy and I have always liked its shape and the unusual pattern around the rim and spout. The yellow is a cheerful colour and my tea pours out of it really well'.

Other objects on show have included a piece of lace, a necklace, a photo, a tapestry cushion, a wooden bowl and a Marmite jar!

3 If the school hall has curtains or blackout facilities, then try having a single slide projected up as the pupils come into and settle down for assembly. Nothing need be said about the image until the end of the week (or whatever number of days is suitable for your purposes). A short statement about what it is and who made it may then be included and a simple 'We hope you have enjoyed looking at it' can be said. Of course, more can be made of it and it can be used to illustrate the focal point of an assembly, but just as a range of interesting music (traditional, modern and classical) is often played to pupils, then so too can images become part of the daily shared experience as well.

I was discussing possible ways of using artefacts with a group of colleagues on a course when a teacher nearing retirement age said, 'I had quite forgotten, we always used to show slides when the children came into assembly years ago', thus proving, as ever, that rarely is anything a completely new idea!

4 Displays acting as a stimulus for looking are covered fully in another book in this series *Creative display and environment* by Margaret Jackson. She makes clear numerous ways in which art and artefacts can be gathered together to provoke and inform and demonstrates how they may be displayed in classrooms and communal areas throughout the school building. It is helpful to re-state the value of using original materials and secondary resources as displays in the context of this book too, since they add to the opportunities that children may have to look and think at their own level and pace.

Increasingly it is becoming apparent that schools are looking afresh at how and where they can expose pupils to artefacts and images in response to the demands of the National Curriculum art document, and displays are obvious routes to explore (see also Figures C10(a) and C10(b) on page 105 in the colour section).

Consistently I witness lively corners where the work of a single artist is on view through the careful arrangement of open books and posters. Decorative pieces and collections unified by content (mother and child, the seasons, landscapes, the urban environment, etc.) are often grouped together to stimulate pupil awareness and knowledge.

Figure 15 Here a corner is enlivened by a display on the theme of 'faces'

Figure 16(b) A seven-year-old works in the same circular format, referring strongly to Avercamp's composition when it suited his needs

Figure 16(a) Winter scene – Avercamp

Within such displays it makes sense to put up children's own work alongside the original stimulus or reference materials including, where appropriate, artefacts. This way the pupils who have produced them can reflect on the connections they have made and other pupils, who have not produced the work, can see if they can identify links and associations.

ACTIVITIES FROM THE CLASSROOM

The following activities show some of the ways in which two-dimensional images can be used in primary classrooms. They all demonstrate interesting approaches, but from observation and/or trialling, I would suggest that they are most meaningful when used as part of a sequence of work. They are rarely fully explored if used as a series of 'one-off' activities. As always, when selecting ways of using art works, we should be clear about what it is we hope the children will learn.

These activities are becoming increasingly commonplace – and indications are given as to where they might be placed within a sequence or unit of work in order to aid planning and to capitalise on their potential. For example, the first two activities could be used as colour matching exercises within a unit of work on colour.

Activity 1

Each pupil is given a paper 'viewfinder' (a shape cut out of a piece of paper) to push across and around an original image until they find a piece that they find visually exciting as a detail and/or mini-composition. Pupils are then asked to paint or draw the chosen section as an enlargement, whilst working in the style of the chosen

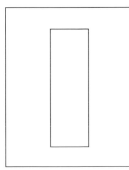
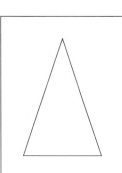
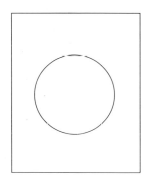

artist. Try experimenting with different-shaped viewfinders – try long and thin, symmetrical, asymmetrical and geometric – which will help to bring home the fact that artists do not always choose to work on a rectangular surface (see diagram on page 69).

Enjoy playing around with ideas. For example, if an equilateral triangular viewfinder, or other appropriate geometrical shape, is chosen, the images can eventually be used to make a class 'net' picture out of the individually (pupil) selected portions. These can be pasted up to create a fresh original piece, which in turn can be the start of pupils looking at the possibilities of random pattern making.

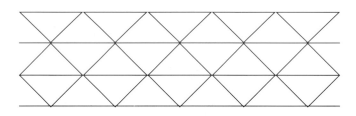

When to use a painting in this context

Plan to use part of a sequence exploring mark-making in paint; investigate smooth and rough paint surfaces. Focus in closely so that marks become more and more abstract in nature, and develop this into a picture made up of abstract patterns which can be exciting because of their unexpected configurations. Launch the sequence with challenges of different ways of making marks with a range of large and small brushes, and large and small glue spreaders or spatulas. Build up layers of paint, and overlap/layer/scratch back through wet top surface to dry surface underneath, etc. Finally, introduce a painting of your choice once these investigations have been made.

Activity 2

Here, pupils do the same as in Activity 1, but with a view to transposing it into a new statement by using a different material. For example, a selected segment is interpreted into a collage piece using a variety of papers. Alternatively, the segment can be transposed into a

Linear diagrams of
Activities 2 and 3

textile piece – a fabric collage or weaving. Page 71 shows an entire image being used in this way, but smaller sections are just as valid. The images developed through circular viewfinders can later be stitched into large-scale pieces using loose-weave material stretched over plastic PE hoops.

Activity 3

With this activity, each pupil is allocated one section of a grid to paint (see page 71). Again, the whole rationale of this activity might be part of a colour mixing/colour matching sequence, or it could be the study of a specific painting style. Choose any image that suits your need, for example one that uses broad brushwork, thick (impasto) use of paint layered on with glue spreaders to echo the use of palette knives or dots of colour (pointilism) used to build up a surface.

Figure C11 on page 106 in the colour section shows a class of seven- and eight-year-olds working in this way, but this again was not an isolated task. The pupils had previously made studies from direct observation of actual sunflowers (before being shown Van Gogh's sunflower image); they had used a variety of graphic media to record the flowerheads and they had made enlargements of the central part of the sunflower as bold, pastel drawings that explored a pattern in nature. The illustrated piece came next, which in turn led on to the poetry work.

Activity 4

Let each pupil select a colour reproduction of an image with just a small section of the image available for the pupils to view. Paperclip a piece of paper over the image that has a window cut out exposing the chosen section (see diagram on page 73). The pupils can then be challenged to extend and develop a picture from this starting point. (Calendars are good sources to find appropriate large-scale reproductions in the numbers required for this.)

There will be no right or wrong outcomes, but pupils should be asked to analyse the portion visible in order to gain as many clues as possible. For example, they should consider whether it is likely to be indoors or out; representational or abstract. For younger children it could be described as a 'subject' or 'likeness' picture or a pattern picture. Ask the children what kinds of colours they can see, and how

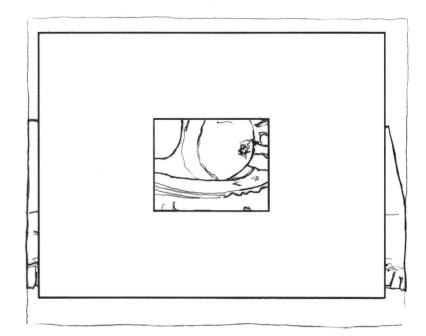

the artist put on the paint. What kind of strokes did he or she use? Could it be part of a subject – a building, landscape or person?

The success of this activity relies on the teacher's selection of the imagery, since it is important to reveal a section that makes bold and obvious indications to the pupil. This again should be in the context of a series of work, and images should be found that exemplify a focus that is being taken at the time (this could be about composition, backgrounds and foregrounds, colour 'families', etc). This approach can create laughter, discussion and declarations of 'mine is a better idea anyway' amongst pupils when the full picture is finally revealed.

Activity 5

Offer each pupil a colour reproduction which has been cut in half and glued to some paper (see diagram on page 74). Another pupil, preferably not working at the same table, can be given the other half. Each pupil is then asked to complete the image working from imagination in such a way as to make the 'join' as invisible as possible (see page 128). This activity could also be part of colour mixing and colour blending work. Any media can be used, but it generally makes sense to select studies in chalks or pastels, for example, at a time when pupils have had time to explore the characteristics of these and are ready to use them in a sustained and considered manner.

A CASE STUDY

The following is an account of a single painting, 'The Birthday' by Marc Chagall. It was used with a class of seven- to nine-year-olds as an open-ended project which lasted nearly a term. The teacher used this one image as the reference point for much learning. In effect, this painting weaved its way in and out of many weeks of work and so became an initial stimulus, a constant source of inspiration, the focus for work on details and aspects of content, and an image to look back on with affection and heightened understanding.

Art and design was the main thrust of the project, but language work, design and technology, dance, mime, music, and social and spiritual aspects were all apparent in a range of lively and thoughtful outcomes. The sequence of work was so impressive that it deserves to be recorded at length. The reader should bear in mind that the following activities took place over many weeks.

Background and development of the project as described by the class teacher

A vivid account of the genesis of the picture, 'The Birthday' (1915), is in the memoirs of Chagall's wife, Bella. She describes a visit to the artist's room; how she found out about the date of his birthday; how she got up early in the morning to pick flowers for Chagall, then ran home to put on her best dress and to collect an armful of colourful scarves and drapes, even the quilt off her bed, and how she hurried across the town to his room. She remembers him rummaging through his canvases, putting one on his easel, and starting to paint straight away.

The introduction to the project is the theme of the picture – birthdays – something every child knows about and loves talking about. We talk about unusual presents, funny incidents, whose birthday it is next and who is the oldest in the class. I show a large poster reproduction of our picture. The following discussion centres around two figures in the picture. Why is the man floating in the air? Where are his arms? The children all agree that the two people in the picture are 'boyfriend and girlfriend' and that they must be in love. We don't quite solve the mystery of the flying figure, but Jordana tells us she always skips and jumps when she is happy, and perhaps the man in the picture is doing the same – only higher.

Answering the question, 'Did you paint this, Miss?' I tell the class about Marc Chagall and his early life in the small town of Vitebsk. I talk about the Jewish community, about his father who was a herring seller, about his early attempts to join the local art school, and the fact that nobody liked his first paintings. Some children nod as if they understand how he must have felt. Then I read an extract to them from Bella Chagall's memoirs. The children ask whether it is a true story, and I tell them it is, and that the picture is proof of this.

We have already established the fact that the painting is a happy one, and go on to talk about other occasions which make people happy. Then we discuss different feelings, for instance, anger, jealousy, surprise and fear. We read a selection of poems dealing with feelings, and then read a wonderful book called *Angry Arthur*, which happens to be Clare's library book. After break, some children write their own poems – all choosing happiness for their theme. The rest of the class mix 'happy' colours and paint beautiful, swirling patterns. Red and pink shades predominate, but Gareth decides grey, black and white make him happy because 'they are smart colours'.

We listen to a selection of Russian music and then discuss the sort of curling, floating shapes which remind us of our picture and which will fit in with the music. The children work in pairs, taking turns to be the leader. The leader invents movements, the partner follows. Then the pairs combine with others to make small groups of four or five. The end result is a combination of mime and dance. We later show our dance to Class 2, who are impressed and ask to see our picture.

There are art books and prints on every table. The children are immediately interested and wonder whether we are looking at different pictures today. And why do we need the hand lenses? We look for interesting patterns in the pictures and sketch a small selection of the ones we like best. Aaron, who is the thinker amongst the first years, finds out that you only need to draw a small part of the pattern, because once you know it you can carry on your own. Well done, Aaron!

A small group of children is busy working from the patterns from our 'Birthday' picture. A plea for scarves and drapes has brought a splendid response. One mother brings in a beautiful hand-embroidered tablecloth and is obviously a little nervous about leaving it. I suggest she stay to see what we are planning to do with it. She watches as I arrange Emma on a chair in the middle of the room. Emma has lovely, thick, curly hair, and when I have finished draping the scarves and lengths of materials around her she looks like a little Romany girl. The children sit around her, sketching, comparing and chatting. The folds of material present some difficulties, but there are many brave attempts to draw them. Charlie's mother starts sketching, and the children are full of admiration. It makes me think that they don't often see us, the adults, reading, painting or drawing.

Half the class, a manageable group of thirteen, are in Christchurch Mansion. We are equipped with clipboards and drawing tools and are hunting for patterns. There are so many that the children are quite bewildered, and we eventually decide to concentrate on one room. Some children draw the beautiful panelling, whilst others concentrate on the patterns present in the bed hangings and the wallpaper. The children are totally absorbed in their tasks, and I feel very proud of them. An attendant comes through the door, 'I didn't know you were here,' he mutters. We take it as a compliment. Tomorrow I will bring the second half of the class here.

Again, the clipboards are in use. Class 5 are swarming all over the school grounds and we are looking for patterns again. We find them on the manhole covers, the bricks, the fence, and the paving stones. Back in the classroom, we transfer the best patterns onto clean paper. Our pattern collection is growing quite impressive.

We are looking at the 'Birthday' picture again – it seems like an old friend now. Westley tells me he had a dream about it, and I ask him what happened in his dream. He giggles a little and says, 'I was eating the food on the table'. We take a closer look at the room in the picture, and I suggest that the children write letters to their friends in Bentley school describing the room to them. A delegation of boys appears at my desk. They are doubtful. 'The Bentley lot wouldn't want to know about it,' says Adam. I can see his point. We decide that anybody who wants to can write their letter to a fictitious friend instead.

We spend the following three afternoons making shoebox models of Chagall's room. Luckily the furniture is quite simple to make, and the older pupils help the younger ones to cut up the fabrics. There is a lively trade in small boxes which the children have brought from home.

The children have some homework to do – they have to draw a plan of their own bedrooms, ten centimetres representing every metre. Next they have to design their ideal bedrooms. They draw the pieces of furniture they would like and use small samples of curtain materials and carpet. They then make a plan showing where they would put everything. Some children have time to draw an 'artist's impression' of their rooms as well.

There is a table in the centre of the classroom with a blue flowered tablecloth, a cake, a purse and a few other items. 'I know,' says Sharne, 'it's the table from the picture.' So it is. The children sit around it in small groups and paint. They are using watercolours today, which they much prefer to ready-mix paint. We talk about the meaning of the phrase 'still life', and the children who finish early look at some still-life pictures in our art book collection. Just before the children go home, we have a small problem to solve. What to do with the cake? Luckily, with a knife and twenty-six hungry children to hand, the solution is not too difficult to find . . .

A collection of small calendar pictures comes in useful at last. We cut out window frames, sills and curtains and use part of the calendar pictures to make 'window' collages. Some children sit a cat on the windowsill, some put vases of flowers and pots of geraniums there. The results are attractive.

We are looking at the 'Birthday' picture again, this time concentrating on the flowers. Some children want to paint a bunch of flowers just like the one in the picture. Another group is making printing blocks out of pieces of cardboard. Were it the right time of year, I would have brought in a bunch of flowers resembling the ones in the painting, as a model for sketching and painting. Later on in the summer we are going to press flowers and use them for collages.

A group of children is looking at my catalogue from the big Chagall exhibition. Many of his pictures show flowers, and we talk about the different occasions when people like to use flowers – at weddings, christenings, funerals, for somebody who is ill, in a button-hole.

I had planned to work on colour with my class, still using our painting as a focal point, but I felt that after all our work the children had reached saturation point. After all, we had achieved a lot more than I had ever expected. 'The Birthday' had provided us with inspiration for our art work (and much more besides) for nearly a term.

Of course, there is no need to go into quite so much detail in order to enjoy a painting; but for us it was right at the time, and the results of our labour justify the many hours spent on the project. I feel the children may, in future, look at paintings with more enjoyment and a deeper understanding than they would have done before we started our work.

5 Art into language – language into art

Art and artefacts can provide a wonderful springboard into storytelling and other language work. The links can mutually benefit both areas of learning and heighten pupil awareness and sensitivity in an exciting way, as the following account will verify.

Recently, I took a group of eight- and nine-year-olds to a museum of rural life, and one of the artefacts that we focused our attention on was a glorious travellers' caravan. We talked about what life might be like travelling on the open road, the sense of freedom, the time it would take to journey from place to place, what one would notice that would be missed in a car or a train and the impact of the weather and the seasons. It was easy conversation – I doubt if there is a child anywhere that would not respond to a caravan of this sort. Its size and scale fascinated them – it was romantic and instantly desirable. Every pupil wanted to sleep inside it and eat sitting on the steps beneath the stars whilst gazing into a crackling fire.

Figure 17   Travellers' wagon

We considered other questions: Who might have made it and when? From what was it made? What were the decorative details images of, why were they chosen and were they the same on other vans? How many people might have lived in it? Details were closely observed and recorded in sketchbooks, and the names of the types of caravans, benders and related ephemera that were on display were noted down from the labels provided. As we sat in a barn to eat our sandwiches, rain started to pelt down noisily. This fed the imagination further: What would such rain sound like inside the van? Would it be warm? How could wet things be dried?

Back at school, the pupils worked from the experience of the visit with their class teacher. Journeys and different kinds of transport were projects for the term, and their class teacher helped to rebuild the caravan in the minds of the children. They wrote stories about an imagined journey, using their sketchbooks to help re-engage their imaginations and recall details. As they developed their writing, they drafted more questions and possibilities: Is it day or night, fine and clear or wet and stormy? Are we travelling on a modern road or on a bumpy track? What can we hear? Is the horse lively and willing or tired at the end of many miles of pulling the caravan? The writing became wonderfully descriptive and extended.

In the meantime, their teacher laid out art materials for use later in the morning. Figures 12(a) and 12(b) on page 107 show two of the outcomes that reflect the intensity of the pupils' experience. The first shows the sun smiling down, just as a carved detail had done on the van itself. The second has a strong narrative line. The nine-year-old girl who designed it was spellbound by the van and wanted to travel in it very much. She imagined herself sitting on a great grinning moon playing music and looking down on the earth below.

> **Because I wouldn't have a TV or a cassette player in my van, I would play a guitar and travel all across the world.**

All too often, illustrations which accompany children's writing are given little status and emerge haphazardly without very much teacher support or stimulus. Materials offered are often limited to an inadequate range of felt-tip pens or poor-quality coloured pencils, the image often being carried out on totally unsuitable lined paper. In this instance the opposite was true. The pupils monoprinted, drew back into the prints, worked further on the surface with chalks and pastels and embellished the results with sequins and other delicate collage materials. Consequently, the work was rich and expressive with vibrant surface qualities that somehow matched well with the subject matter. Both the language and artwork were considered important, both were extended and developed fully and both used the shared starting point of the caravan to great effect. (See Figures C12(a) and C12(b) on page 107 in the colour section.)

The teacher's role was vital in managing the experience to achieve these ends and to ensure that results of quality emerged in both curriculum areas. However, without the original artefact as a stimulus, work showing such pupil involvement is unlikely to have come about. Later, the teacher remarked that he had been able to use the caravan in many more ways than he had first imagined and that he was particularly pleased that it had given him the opportunity to talk about a minority group that is often marginalised within our society, in a way that respected their culture, traditions and skills.

USING THE SPOKEN WORD

The pleasures and value of listening to the spoken word and oral storytelling traditions are widely acknowledged. Many people prefer the radio to the television or cinema screen because it allows them to create personal visions of character or place undefined by another's interpretation. But as the radio becomes a less dominant feature in many contemporary households (and may well be totally absent), teachers can sometimes be the only people that children hear reading or telling stories.

Indeed, I found it interesting when teaching in the secondary sector some years ago that, on asking the eleven- and twelve-year-olds if, after a term at their new school, there was anything they missed about primary school, a large number said 'being read to'. As a result, I, and a number of other teachers arranged to spend one lunchtime a week reading stories, with pupils free to come and listen if they wanted to. We were amazed at how many turned up, even when it was a warm and wind-free day outside!

To use stories and poems as a way of launching pupils into making paintings, drawings, collages and prints is a well-established practice, and I recently saw a delightfully funny set of paintings which were a direct result of just such an approach. A class of seven- and eight-year-olds had been reading Roald Dahl's *The Twits*, and the pictures were wonderful visual explorations of Mr Twit's beard. The writing had undoubtedly appealed to every child's love of the vulgar and distasteful, and their teacher had capitalised on this by asking the pupils to show the most messy and disgusting beards possible. Each piece of paper was filled, like a close-up frame in a film, with a large open mouth dribbling an array of foodstuffs into spiky, thick hair. Each one was very different, with the children appearing to compete with each other to place the most revolting globules of half-masticated delicacies in and around, between and under every hair. The teacher had wrung every drop out of the descriptive passage '. . . make soggy shapes, things that ooze and drip, where are the dry crumby bits? . . .' and as a result, the paintings were a riot of colour and textures. These challenges lead quite naturally into the children looking at the work of illustrators and making judgements as to whether they have successfully communicated the content and expressed the mood.

Younger children can respond just as fully when the right encouragement is given. Figure 18 shows a five-year-old's drawing of 'Peter laughing at the flowers' from a story in a Leila Berg book. The teacher of this class said that the children adored this book and drew readily, and with great affection, their images of naughty Peter up to his various antics. Figure C13 on page 108 in the colour section shows a four-year-old's image of the same incident. It is fascinating to note how the five-year-old thinks of the flowers in ordered rows, with the bees approaching in gleeful anticipation, whilst the four-year-old's garden is a blaze of irregularly placed sweeps of colour. Each has internalised the story in their own unique way and offered images that are totally different yet equally valid.

Figure 18 'Peter laughing at the flowers'

STORIES WITHIN PICTURES AND OTHER ARTEFACTS

Paintings, drawings and prints are perhaps the most obvious source to find stories being told, which also makes them a rich resource for the humanities – history, geography and religious studies. A battle recorded, scenes from the life of Christ or the Buddha or other religious figures, children playing, Indian godesses, shipwrecks and other disasters, mythological beasts, legends and allegorical tales are but a few of the subjects artists have traditionally explored throughout the centuries. There are, however, many more resources one can use for storytelling purposes. Murals and frescoes, sculptures and carvings, painted ceilings (the Sistine Chapel is a wonderful source of storytelling on a grand scale), stained glass windows, mosaics and textile pieces (the Bayeaux Tapestry, Egyptian rugs and carpets from the Eastern world) can all recall human beliefs and struggles, clan and tribal histories and record moments in stories, real or imagined. (See Figure C14 on page 108 in the colour section.)

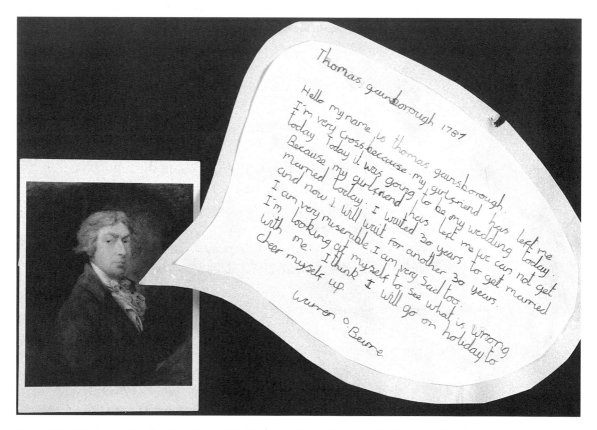

Figure 19   Work resulting from a visit to Gainsborough House Museum. Children used archive material and produced speech bubbles from information researched. Here an eight-year-old was able to see Gainsborough's writing desk and read some of his letters

It can sometimes be fun to take one story, for example St George and the Dragon, and research it to see just how many ways the same tale has been told by a number of different artists. The School's Library Service, given enough warning, may well be prepared to do such a task on your behalf, and it is a lovely way, yet again, to prove to pupils that there are many approaches and solutions to the same problem.

To work from the world of the pupils outwards is, as has been said before, a powerful and realistic way of working. Aspects of visual storytelling within the culture of even the youngest children – that is the world of cartoons, animation and comic books – can be used as a direct lead into looking at other stories told in sequences. Pupils can be shown diptych and triptych (two- and three-panelled pictures) as formats for staged storytelling. They can be shown medieval manuscripts depicting related scenes from monastic life and the long handscroll format favoured by the Chinese and Japanese and can be invited to work in similar ways themselves.

For animators, strip cartoonists, designers of comic strips and originators of television advertisements, storyboarding is central to the creative process. Each shot or idea is roughed out on paper, the storyline is broken down into essential visual content, and the angle (view) from which it is to be taken is decided. Parallels exist in all these arenas of work and they all utilise filming devices such as the pan shot, the zoom shot and the close up. Often the artist will exploit images being in or out of focus to indicate speed and movement. Other conventions are evident – virtually all children appear to know how to express a 'bang', 'pow' or 'zap' effectively!

A little while ago, I began a project with a class of ten- and eleven-year-olds. We started by collecting comics and comic books (it was the most rapidly gathered collection I have ever experienced) to look at the storytelling process in an analytical way. The pupils worked in groups in order to think about how the storytelling was broken down, to identify what kinds of viewpoints (aerial, close-up, distorted, etc.) were evident and to try to work out if there were ways that showed time was passing. They were also asked to note the regular and irregular divisions and sub-divisions of the pages.

The brief was then set. Each pupil had to create a comic page layout depicting either: *(a)* the moment they woke up until the moment they arrived at the school gates; or *(b)* the moment they left school until the time that they got into bed at night. It was winter time and I deliberately chose a time sequence that would either start or end in darkness.

Jointly we drafted lists of possible mini-incidents that might occur within this time span and we allowed for artistic licence and gross exaggeration (in the spirit of all good work in this field), but we agreed to stay within the bounds of reason and 'reality'.

As part of the initial stimulus, we also looked at the Raymond Briggs' books *Father Christmas, Father Christmas goes on Holiday* and *When the Wind Blows.* With *The Snowman,* we looked at the book and then watched the animated version, comparing and contrasting techniques and devices used in both. These books and the film are sheer joy and show all the concepts that I was asking the pupils to explore carried out with endless skill, humour, subtlety and care. Certainly the class was bowled over by the amount of detail apparent in the pictures, and this seemed to have the effect of their setting higher standards for themselves within their own work (see Figures 20(a) and (b) for two examples).

Figure 20(a)

Figures 20(a) & (b)   Storyboarding

Figure 20(b)

6 Implementation and development

Art is a separate, discrete subject within the National Curriculum, and, as such, it should have adequate time allocated to it within the school week. The entitlement that pupils have is to a continuous, planned progression of work throughout their primary years which should allow all children to encounter a full range of experiences, to include time spent handling paint, drawing with different graphic media, printmaking, collage work, textiles and three-dimensional materials. There are many opportunities when it is valuable for children to see the natural linkage of their own work to that of artists, designers and craftworkers, but these should never be forced. There are also some areas of experience where practical exploration, personal communication and expression should be seen as a pure art experience, for example:

- when pupils are being introduced to a new skill, technique or process (including the use of information technology software);
- when pupils are exploring and investigating materials new to them so that they may discover their qualities, properties, limitations and possibilities (for the very young child, 'structured play' is vital to the learning process);
- when pupils are stimulated to work from their own memories, imaginations and feelings;
- when pupils are dealing with problem-solving situations that require individual research and investigations – and at any other time you believe it not to be an appropriate focus.

REVIEWING THE PLACE OF ARTEFACTS IN OUR CURRICULUM

Deciding when and where to use art and artefacts within the teaching programme is the first step in successful planning. It may be necessary to move through various stages in the planning process, and this might mean that broad and direct questions are asked, at least in the initial stages of implementation:

- Do we use art, design and craftwork in our teaching?
- How frequently do we use them and in which contexts?
- Are we resourced enough to do so?
- Have we given/do we need to give a coordinating role to any one individual?
- Do we need to develop any whole-school approaches in relation to the use of art and artefacts, including taking account of any financial implications?
- Do we need to build into the medium- and long-term planning staff needs and in-service training requirements so that we can be effective in our teaching when referencing through original art and artefacts and related secondary resource materials?
- What self-help strategies can be employed?

To find out if, when and how art and artefacts are being used is obviously best undertaken as a whole-school review. Staff meetings may need to be arranged, or time within professional development days allocated in order to discover 'where we are now' and 'where we hope to be in the future'. If such broad planning is not carried out initially as a whole-school activity, then there is a danger that some areas of study will be too frequently visited and some not visited at all. I sometimes wonder if there are pupils who will leave school believing that the world of art and design consists of about five paintings, an African mask and a Greek urn! There is nothing wrong in using Van Gogh's 'Sunflowers' and 'Starry Night' (witness their effective use in the examples contained in this book), Monet's water lilies and a distorted Picasso head, *but* if this is the selection offered to pupils at the age of five and six and is all that remains on offer until pupils leave school at age sixteen or eighteen, then we will not have revealed much to them concerning the delights of the visual and tactile world, and their sense of heritage will be meagre indeed!

Some schools have taken a very straightforward and painless route in order to discover what is really being achieved. Agreement has been made that every time any art, design or craftwork is done, every teacher in every year group will put one example of it into a folder that they keep in their room. Three-dimensional work (again just one representative piece) is photographed, using a shared school camera, and added to the folder. Care is taken to select different pupils' work to add to the collection so that no one individual is robbed of ownership of their work.

The aim behind this agreement is that, at the end of term, or an entire academic year, each member of staff brings their folder to a staff meeting (held in the school hall to allow for the laying out of the work on the floor) for a 'show and tell' session. It then becomes immediately apparent to all if a fair balance is being met, if breadth of coverage is sound or if one discipline or experience or type of imagery is heavily used at the expense of neglect elsewhere. If an imbalance is detected, then steps can be taken to correct this the following term.

There is much that can be gained from using this strategy:

- it provides instant evidence of the pupils' actual experiences;
- it helps staff identify patterns within their own teaching which they might not otherwise have realised;
- it makes clear what planning needs to be done for the future in the light of progression and continuity (apparent or absent!);
- it allows teachers to share and learn from each other's approaches and expertise in a direct and supportive way.

This book is not intended to give a comprehensive picture of all that a child's art education should encompass, but if this particular idea is adopted, it does, by definition, reveal all that is happening. For example, some schools have found it useful to realise that 'We all seem to be good at observational drawing, but very little work from the imagination is being carried out . . . Many of us have units of work on colour, but not in such a way that challenges are set for the older pupils . . . We do too much pattern work and not enough printmaking', etc. (See Figure C15(a) and C15(b) on page 109.)

Once an accurate picture of the current situation emerges, then it is possible to make informed decisions about what is needed next. If

such a person does not already exist, then it is at this point
(particularly in the case of a large school) that one or two people need
to take (or be given!) responsibility for developing ideas, resources
and opportunities to meet the pupils' needs. The energies of one or
more teachers can make an enormous difference to any area of the
curriculum about which they feel a particular passion. Time and
again I have seen this in action and have marvelled at the
developments one person's enthusiasm and initiative can make in a
school. A knock-on effect takes place as work of vigour and depth
begins to appear and as others feel they have someone to turn to for
inspiration and guidance. Any schemes of work, or plans for units of
study, are always more successful when they are negotiated and not
merely imposed, but a sensitive and lively coordinator has a vital role
to play in offering a broad framework that everyone can understand
and feel able to participate within.

In the context of developing resources and making contacts in
order to strengthen teaching using art and artefacts, teachers may find
the following helpful.

WHO, WHERE, WHAT?

The following list of groups (see page 92) may assist teachers in
considering the potential of artists, craftworkers, and designers in
their own locality. Turn to Chapter 2 for ideas on how to set up and
use residencies and other ways of using artists, designers or
craftworkers in schools.

There is an obvious overlap with design and technology in the
work carried out by many of these people, and contact with them
may mean two areas of the curriculum can be covered simultaneously.

It may be sensible to use such a list (adding any others you can
think of) and send it with a 'Do you know, or do you know someone
who knows . . . ?' letter out to governors and parents to see if the start
of a mini-school directory of possible contacts can be started. Many
practitioners are either very busy, very poor or very shy, but few turn
out not to be 'education friendly', and they may well be open to the
idea of visiting schools or having pupils visit them. At the same time,
ask colleagues to reflect on their own families and friends   the local
signwriter, textile worker or blacksmith may just turn out to be a
drinking partner in the pub down the road.

WHO MAKES ART, CRAFT AND DESIGN?

Painters

Sculptors

Printmakers

Potters

Ceramicists

Fashion designers

Theatre designers

Jewellery designers -
  silversmith
  goldsmith
  enameller

Textile designers -
  spinners
  weavers
  fabric printers
  knitters
  hatters
  batik artists

Architects

Interior designers

Landscape designers

Exhibition designers

Woodcarvers

Woodturners

Stonemasons

Glass makers

Stained glass window designers

Photographers

Film/video makers

Animators

Television designers

Computer software designers

Illustrators

Calligraphers

Papermakers

Bookbinders

Leather workers

Saddlers

Basket makers

Toymakers

Puppet makers

Musical instrument makers

Dollshouse makers

Wrought iron workers

Industrial designers

Furniture designers

Product designers

Package designers

Graphic designers

Depending on the geographical location of individual schools, other possibilities may exist. Try making contact with local (large or small) galleries asking for their programme of events for the coming year to aid planning, and any recommendations that they may be prepared to give concerning locally based artists and designers. Ask if it is possible to be included on the invitation list to private views in order to make direct contact with artists.

It is also worth trying local high or upper schools and asking for dates of GCSE and A-level examinations and if it is possible to plan a visit with pupils, preferably at a time when the students could be around to welcome younger pupils and to talk about their work. Providing you are sensitive enough to stay well away when public examinations are being moderated, then any high-school colleague is likely to welcome this as part of good liaison arrangements. Many are prepared to go much further, and there exist lovely links where high-school pupils have worked in primary schools (and vice versa) and where art work from older students, including sketchbooks, logs and research sheets, have been lent for display and stimulation purposes. (See Figure C16(a), (b), (c), and (d) on pages 110–11 in the colour section.) Make contact with your local art school and/or art department within a local college or university and ask the same questions. Dates of diploma and/or degree shows are known well in advance and are often, just as in schools, glorious, diverse celebrations of youthful achievements.

These local facilities, where they exist, are sometimes within walking or public transport distance and free to enter by arrangement. They provide realistic ways for pupils to encounter original works of art and design comparatively easily. The definition of 'appropriate artists to reference' in primary schools does not always have to include the Masters – the aspiring have much to offer too!

Local links can be added to by contacting outside agencies. Where available in your region/local authority, the following have extensive contacts and are there to help:

- LEA specialist advisory support;
- Regional Arts Boards;
- Regional Craft Societies;
- Regional Arts Centres.

Funding arrangements of the above agencies are under constant review and/or in a state of change, but it is worth enquiring if any financial support is available from the last three listed. Similarly, many LEAs have lively industry/business/school links that may be able to offer sponsorship for artist/designer/craftworker residencies in schools or other related projects.

Bibliography

Adam, E. and Ward, C., *Art and the Built Environment*, Harlow, Longman, 1982

Benton, Michael and Peter, *Double Vision*, London, Hodder and Stoughton, published in association with The Tate Gallery, 1990

Berg, Leila, *Little Pete Stories*, London, Penguin, 1959

Briggs, Raymond, *Father Christmas*, London, Penguin, 1973

Briggs, Raymond, *Father Christmas goes on Holiday*, London, Penguin, 1975

Briggs, Raymond, *The Snowman*, London, Penguin, 1978

Briggs, Raymond, *When the Wind Blows*, London, Penguin, 1978

Charlton, Tony, *Guide to Courses and Careers in Art, Craft and Design*, Wiltshire, NSEAD, 1989

Dahl, Roald, *The Twits*, London, Penguin, 1980

Dust, Karen and Sharp, Caroline, *Artists in Schools, a Handbook for Teachers and Artists*, London, Bedford Square Press, 1990

Gombrich, E.H., *The Story of Art*, London, The Phaidon Press, 1964

Hampshire County Council, *Further Guidelines for Art Education*, 1992

Jackson, Margaret, *Creative display and environment*, London, Hodder and Stoughton, 1993

Jameson, Kenneth, *Pre-school and Infant Art*, London, Studio Vista Ltd, 1968

Leicht, Hermann, *History of the World's Art*, London, Spring Books, 1963

Morgan, Margaret, *Art 4–11*, Oxford, Blackwells, 1988; London, Simon and Schuster, 1992

Morgan, Margaret, *Art in Practice, Motivation and Development*, Wantage, Oxfordshire, Nash Pollock Publishing, 1993

Oram and Kitanura, *Angry Arthur*, London, Penguin, presently out of print; to be reprinted in January 1995

Peppin, Anthea, *The National Gallery Children's Book*, London, Publications Department, The National Gallery, 1983

Richardson, Marion, *Art and the Child*, London, University of London Press Ltd, 1948

Sedgwick, Dawn and Fred, *Drawing to learn*, London, Hodder and Stoughton, 1993

Taylor, Rod, *Educating For Art, Critical Response and Development*, Harlow, Longman, 1986

The Ironbridge Gorge Museum and Shropshire Education Department, *Under-Fives and Museums, Guidelines for Teachers*, Ironbridge Gorge Museum Trust, Telford, Shropshire, 1989

Thistlewood, David, *Critical Studies in Art and Design Education*, Harlow, Longman/NSEAD, 1989

Colour section – children's art from four to eleven

Figures C1(a) & (b) A five-year-old boy works with great concentration, having spent a considerable amount of time looking at the work of both Pablo Picasso and Vincent Van Gogh

Figure C1(a)

Figure C1(b)

Figures C2(a)–(d) Ten- and eleven-year-old pupils work with torn and dyed papers to make collaged images from the sculpture of Sophie Ryder

Figure C2(a)

Figure C2(b)

Figure C2(c)

Figure C2(d)

Figure C3(a)

Figure C3(b)

Figure C3(c)

Figure C3(d)

Figures C3(a)–(d)   Displays always enrich the learning environment, and here a range of artefacts and secondary source materials are combined to stimulate a multicultural approach to textile work

Figure C4(a)   An eleven-year-old boy stands amongst the Diwali celebration floor piece ...

Figure C4(b)   ... and a green figure dances amongst swathes of colour ...

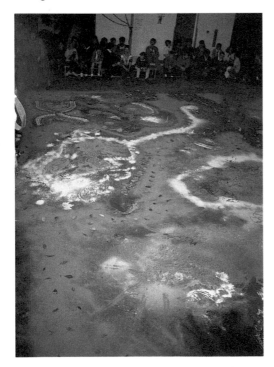

Figure C4(c)   ... whilst the work is admired ...

Figure C4(d)   ... especially the Rangoli patterns

Figure C5(a)

Figure C5(b)

Figures C5(a) & (b)   Children work with craftworkers during a 'hands-on' artists' and craftworkers' day in a primary school. Figure C5(a) shows calligraphy skills being tried, whilst in Figure C5(b) we see another pupil being shown how to card

Figure C6(a)

Figures C6(a) & (b)   Images enlarged from book-based research prior to a museum visit

Figure C6(b)

Figure C7 Shallow dishes made after initial research shown in Figures C6(a) and (b) and information gathered from original artefacts in the museum

Figure C8 A nine-year-old uses a sketchbook to reference from small sections of paintings of his choice, to explore sponge and large brush marks and to make charts of colours that he identified from paintings studied

Figure C9 An eleven-year-old makes an oil pastel drawing after seeing the shelter drawings of Henry Moore produced during the war

A corner display (Figure C10(a)) shows some of the secondary source materials used to stimulate the work on show in the school hall. Here (Figure C10(b)) the stimuli and the children's imagery – paintings, fabric collages and prints – are hung alongside each other for everyone to enjoy

Figure C10(a)

Figure C10(b)

Figure C11   Pupils explore the painting techniques and colour range of Van Gogh in individual panels prior to assembling as a large group piece

Figures C12(a) & (b)   Two nine-year-olds work from the original stimulus of a travellers' ornate and carved wagon. Figure C12(a) shows an image inspired by a decorative detail on the wagon, and Figure C12(b) shows the image one pupil would paint on the door if the wagon belonged to her

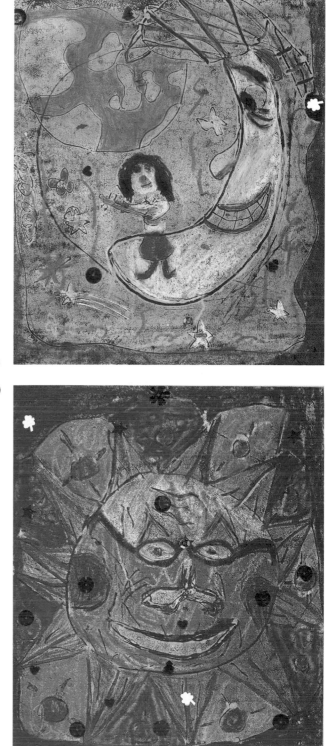

Figure C12(a)

Figure C12(b)

Figure C13   A four-year-old responds to a favourite story in wax crayon and coloured pencils

Figure C14   A six-year-old makes an image of a Viking ship after animated storytelling and much enthusiastic encouragement from the teacher

Figures C15(a) & (b) show prints made by ten-year-olds after studying different fonts and typefaces. The letter collections gathered as part of the pupils' research are made into lively collages prior to the printmaking activity

Figure C15(a)

Figure C15(b)

Figures C16(a)–(d)   It can be very valuable for primary-aged children to see the work of older students. Here, A-level and GCSE students have been making two- and three-dimensional responses to the work of Matisse, and any young pupil is likely to become excited and motivated by the sheer diversity of outcomes produced here

Figure C16(a)
... large-scale card sculpture
... a ceramic piece

Figure C16(b)
... a fan (card and wooden spills)

Figure 16(c)
... batik panel on silk

Figure 16(d)
... a painting

Figure C17   After looking at anatomical drawings by Leonardo da Vinci and some contemporary human biology books, including a wonderful 'pop-up' version, seven- and eight-year-olds construct 'Lazy Bones'

Figure C18   Large-scale group pastel and chalk drawings in the style of Modigliani. This formed part of a sequence of work that included a museum visit and the modelling of clay heads exploring the elongated necks and head shapes characteristic of Modigliani

Figure C19 After discussion about faces and feelings, and looking at the work of Munch (in particular the famous painting 'The Scream') a six-year-old makes his own striking image of pain and anguish

Figure C20(a)   Kandinsky painting
'Improvisation 26 (Rowing) 1912'

Figure C20(b)

Figure C20(c)

Figures C20(b) & (c)   Two special needs pupils spend a long time
looking, mixing colours and making marks in the style of Kandinsky

Figure C21   Sometimes a class's best resource is their teacher. Here a teacher shares
her own work with pupils and makes a seductive display of her source materials,
photographic references and sketchbooks, alongside a weaving

Figure C22   A five-year-old makes a stunning drawing of a playground scene after looking closely at the work of Lowry. He returned to his drawing for a number of days, so strong was his desire to add more and more action

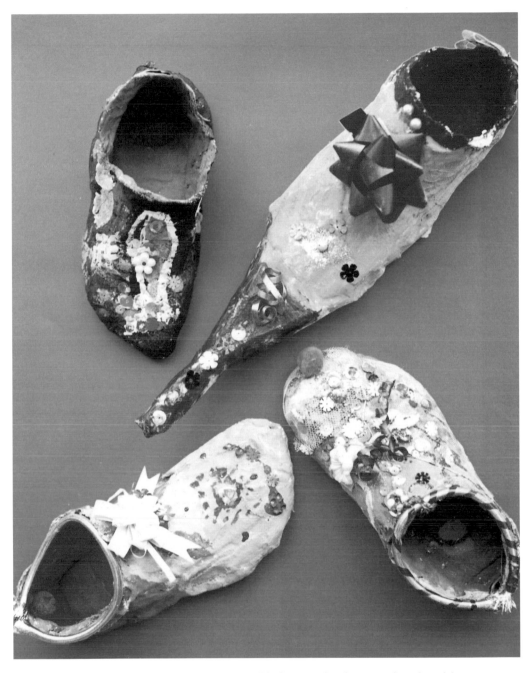

Figure C23   Six- and seven-year-olds design and make painted modroc (plaster-impregnated bandage) shoes. This formed part of a sequence of work that included observational drawings of shoes, after first grouping them into types, and printmaking from soles, as well as researching footwear in medieval imagery, Gainsborough family group portraits and other paintings

Figure C24(a)

Figure C24(b)

Figure C24(c)

Michael Rothenstein (Figure C24(a)) was a printmaker who also enjoyed painting over and around his prints. A ten-year-old works on top of one of Rothenstein's prints (Figure C24(b)) in the same manner as the artist himself might have done. The boy was particularly impressed with the heads of the two punk characters and used colour with care in this part of the image. A nine-year-old preferred to collage over the same part of the print (Figure C24(c)) with heads that were more meaningful to her. The rest of the image she painted and collaged with great gusto

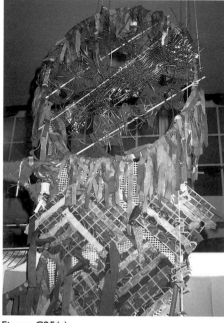

Figure C25(a)

Figure C25(b)

Figure C25(c)

Figure C25(d)

Figures C25(a)–(d)   These show a large-scale group piece, worked on by pupils aged between four and nine years of age during an art week that was devoted to textile work of all kinds. The pupils were shown the works of some professional contemporary textile artists and absorbed some of their techniques and approaches into their own piece

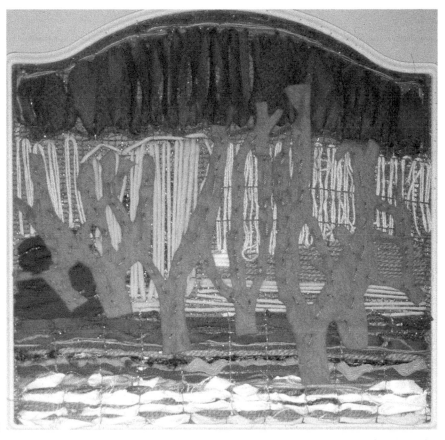

Figure C26(a)

Figure C26(a) shows an eight-year-old pupil's work produced during the same art week. She studied the painting of Paul Signac (Figure C26(b)) and transposed the piece into weaving and threadwork, whilst taking care to match the colour and mood of the original. She was encouraged, however, to modify and amend the original composition to her own liking

Figure C26(b)

Figure C27(a)

Figures C27(a) & (b)   Two eleven-year-olds record from the local environment using wax crayons and oil pastels

Figure C27(b)

Figure C28   Nine- and ten-year-olds make a study of gargoyles and then design their own using clay

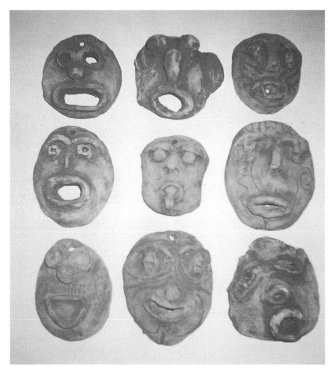

Figure C29(a)

Figure C29(b)

Figures C29(a)–(c)   Three six-year-olds work in the open air using watercolour boxes. The images were made of Ely Cathedral after looking at studies of buildings made by Claude Monet and John Piper

Figure C29(c)

Figure C30(a)

Figures C30(a) & (b)   The fine quality
of much of the work produced for
GCSE and A-level examinations can be
a rich resource for primary schools to
use. These Figures show an
exciting sixth form 'box' project with
accompanying research/sketchbook

Figure C30(b)

Figure C31(a)

Figure C31(b)

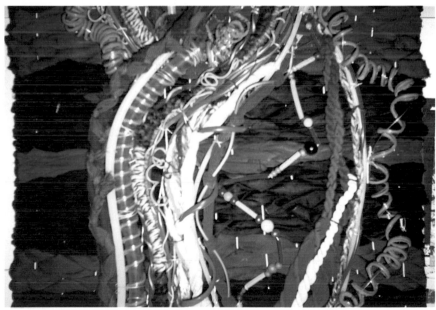

Figure C31(c)

Figure C31(b) shows eight- and nine-year-old pupils using the work of GCSE students to extend their thinking prior to carrying out textile work of their own. They look closely at the pieces shown in Figures C31(a) & (c) and record their responses in their own sketchbooks

Figure C32(a)

Figure C32(b)

Figures C32(a) & (b)   A six-year-old looks closely at a Matisse image and matches the strength and vibrancy of colour apparent in the original

Figures C33(a) & (b) Variety is important, and children should have the opportunity to experience many different kinds and styles of painting in order to discover their preferences. In Figure C33(a), a five-year-old works in the style of Jackson Pollock, whilst in Figure C33(b), a seven-year-old works in the style of Vincent Van Gogh

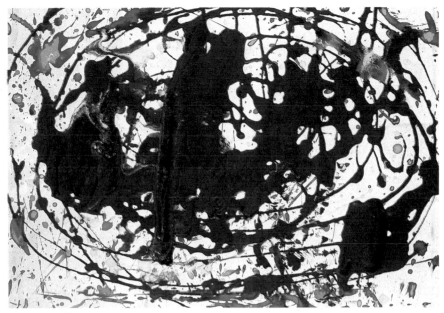

Figure C33(a)

Figure C33(b)

Figure C34(a)

Figure C34(b)

Figures C34(a) & (b)   Two eight-year-olds being challenged to blend colour in such a way as to make the join between their work and the reproduction as invisible as possible